The Great Happiness

BY THE SAME AUTHOR

L'homme qui ne voulait pas être pape. Histoire secrète d'un règne, Albin Michel, 2014; Pluriel, 2018.

Un temps pour mourir. Derniers jours de la vie des moines, Fayard, 2018; Pluriel, 2019; Cardinal Lustiger Prize, Grand Prize of the French Academy.

Trois jours et trois nuits. Le grand voyage des écrivains à l'abbaye de Lagrasse, sous la direction de Nicolas Diat, Fayard-Julliard, 2021; Pluriel, 2022.

Ce qui manque à un clochard, Robert Laffont, 2021; Pocket, 2023.

Les Écrivains sous les drapeaux. Cinq jours avec les régiments des troupes de marine, sous la direction de Nicolas Diat, Fayard, 2022.

Le cœur ne se divise pas. Conversation sur l'unité, avec François Bustillo and Edgar Peña, Fayard, 2023.

WITH CARDINAL ROBERT SARAH:

Dieu ou rien. Entretien sur la foi, Fayard, 2015; Pluriel, 2016.

La Force du silence. Contre la dictature du bruit, Fayard, 2016; Pluriel, 2017; Spirituality Today Prize from the Mediterranean Center of Literature.

Le soir approche et déjà le jour baisse, Fayard, 2019; Pluriel, 2020.

THE GREAT HAPPINESS

Life of the Monks

Nicolas Diat

Our Sunday Visitor
Huntington, Indiana

29 28 27 26 25 24   1 2 3 4 5 6 7 8 9

Our Sunday Visitor Publishing Division
Our Sunday Visitor, Inc.
200 Noll Plaza
Huntington, IN 46750
1-800-348-2440

ISBN: 978-1-63966-184-8 (Inventory No. T2884)
eISBN: 978-1-63966-185-5
LCCN: 2024941330

Cover design and interior design: Amanda Falk
Cover art: Cover image © Private collection of the author

PRINTED IN THE UNITED STATES OF AMERICA

To all the priests of my childhood

Contents

Foreword

Out There, in the Countryside

The road winds in serpentine paths that follow the course of the Black River. Upon arriving from Châtellerault, in France, a town lacking in picturesque charm, the landscape transforms after Tournon-Saint-Martin. The vast, monotonous expanses give way to forests, ponds, and the enclosures of ancient farms. On this peaceful Sunday in June 2019, I came to see those who were once called the black monks.

The Benedictine abbey stands at the forefront of the village; the walker gazes in awe at the tall enclosing walls, the massive bell tower, the long abbey church, and the orchards that watch over the cemetery.

I was familiar with Fontgombault. In winter, the evening falls quickly, and the wind plays in the trees. Fog lingers over the land for a long time.

For the moment, the pastures, paths, and woods held the charm of pocket-sized countries. On the radio, a heatwave was being announced. In a few days, the church would become a refuge for the faithful seeking God and for vacationers escaping the heat.

The monastery is home to around sixty monks. They came from Solesmes in May 1948 to revitalize the contemplative life. Since then, Fontgombault has established and restored six other monasteries.

How can we understand these men shrouded in mystery? Can words truly express what is primarily an inner journey? They had warned me, without mincing words: "Your task will not be simple."

Often, I've watched, fascinated, as the monks set out on an afternoon stroll. Passing through the concealed gate of the orchard, the monks' figures disappear into the countryside. They walk swiftly, in small groups, with a rhythmic pace. Their rough black woolen garments, the traditional tunics of Saint Benedict's followers, create strange and impressive forms. They move forward, laugh, and playfully quarrel. The monks are happy. On these exceptional days, they engage in long conversations, because silence is typically a golden rule.

The seven daily offices, along with matins celebrated at night, form the backbone of an unchanging daily routine. It endures until death. At night, they rise at 4:30 in the morning. Matins, lauds, prime, terce, sext, none, vespers, and compline repeat themselves, day after day, season after season.

The beautiful abbey, that stone vessel whose sanctuary has never collapsed, the refectory with its heavy furnishings and magnificent vaults, the sound of water crashing against the dam, once a mill, the exquisite statue of Our Lady of a Good Death, the boundless gardens — all have weathered the vicissitudes of history. The sole backdrop to monastic lives remains motionless, astonishingly frozen.

The Benedictines love their monastery. A vocation is always tied to a land, a geography, a history. I cannot forget the words of Father Bernard, who so beautifully told me: "If we're absent for a few days, upon our return the church appears even more beautiful. In winter the sanctuary walls are powdered with golden dust. Slanting light floods the abbey. In summer the sun is higher; a mysterious darkness envelops the structure."

The monk flees the ephemeral variety of the world. For him, change is artificial, and monotony a method. Asceticism prepares the soul for contemplation.

I wanted to know if happiness is possible in these seemingly constricted lives. It wasn't a challenge, rather a daring wager: Would sadness and sorrow not be the anticipated horizon for bodies and minds constrained by shackles from time immemorial? At first glance, one might believe that one must be mad or unbalanced to become a monk.

In the dark night, the fathers responsible for waking the community knock on the doors of the cells and invite residents to prayer by exclaiming: "*Benedicamus Domino!* – Let us bless the Lord!" The poor brother, barely awake, says, "*Deo gratias!* – Let us give thanks to God!" The conversation carries on: "*Laudetur Jesus Christus!* – Praise be to Jesus Christ!" The response follows, "*Amen!* – So be it!"

The monk's first words of the long day are a declaration of faith. From 5:00 in the morning until 8:45 in the evening, when the utter silence of the night comes to an end, the monk doesn't speak. They sing matins, lauds, and prime. They celebrate or serve the Mass, recite the Rosary. But they remain silent.

This life might seem humanly impossible. There are plenty of obstacles. Yet, the monks of Fontgombault radiate joy. The light in their gaze is not deceiving. It's a simple happiness.

Because contemplatives are not demigods. They are men who choose to direct their days toward God.

Their schedule is an exhilarating journey. It cannot be measured.

The brothers consider that monastic life can be divided into three periods. The early years have the charm of youth and passion. Then, in the middle of life, the struggle becomes difficult. Doubts, fatigue, and tears are not uncommon. As the end approaches, days pass quickly. The daily routine becomes delightful, and the wise old monk laughs at everything. Just as in the novitiate, he remembers the phrase from the *Rule of Saint Benedict* that asks his followers to "keep death daily before one's eyes." Thus the Benedictine must "watch over the actions of his life at all times and consider that God is always watching us wherever we are."*

"So many hands to transform this world, so few eyes to contemplate it,"† writes Julien Gracq in *Lettrines*. Monks do not belong to that type of men. They are the result of a subtle alchemy that transforms the world through hidden actions. They observe it in silence. Perhaps this is the first secret of their happiness: discretion.

When entering a monastery, one must abandon the world's criteria. The monk is a stripped-down man, focused on heavenly realities, detached from earthly matters. Their life is no longer ours.

To better depict them, we can draw on the first psalm:

Blessed is the man
who walks not in the counsel of the wicked,
nor stands in the way of sinners,

---

* *Rule of Saint Benedict*, trans. Germain Morin from the abbey of Maredsous, revised and annotated from the translation of Philibert Schmitz, 2020 (http://la.regle.org/).

† Julien Gracq, *Lettrines*, Paris, J. Corti, 1967.

nor sits in the seat of scoffers,
but his delight is in the law of the Lord,
and on his law he meditates day and night.

He is like a tree
planted by streams of water,
that yields its fruit in its season,
and its leaf does not wither.
In all that he does, he prospers. (Psalm 1:1–3)

The psalm begins with the word "blessed." It could be misinterpreted. It's not about superficial happiness. It doesn't last the duration of a passion, an intense feeling, or an intoxication. Nevertheless, let's reiterate, monks are human beings. Sorrows and grief don't vanish on the day of taking vows or solemn professions. The idyllic image of a saintly monk ascetic, perpetually lost in the clouds, is far from reality. A Benedictine can stumble on the difficult path of monastic life. The vision of a soft, unattainable, distant life is misleading. The motto of a follower of Saint Benedict is simple: *ora et labora* ("Pray and work").

True happiness is not traded in a monastery like it is in the outside world. Step by step, by constantly revisiting his work, the monk seeks the good, the right, the just. *The Rule of Saint Benedict* is an unending pursuit of balance. Balance of the heart, balance of the intellect, balance of the soul. To achieve this, the monk shuns the wicked, the impure, the indulgent, and the greedy. Nothing grandiose. But the struggle is demanding.

Monastic life will always keep its secret. Love is a matter of the heart; it can't be told, it must be lived. The Little Prince is not wrong: One sees clearly only with the heart. In any case, we will endeavor to follow the path of the monks, that of wise happiness.

The words of the John the Evangelist are well-known:

> The next day again John was standing with two of his disciples; and he looked at Jesus as he walked, and said, "Behold, the Lamb of God!" The two disciples heard him say this, and they followed Jesus. Jesus turned, and saw them following, and said to them, "What do you seek?" And they said to him, "Rabbi" (which means Teacher), "where are you staying?" He said to them, "Come and see." (John 1:35–39)

Come and see Fontgombault ... oh, there won't be anything spectacular. But our hearts will warm. A small mysterious grace will blow. We will watch the light pass through the abbey, the trees in the orchards dancing in the wind, the monks walking in the distance, toward the hills. Gregorian chant will rise to mystical heights. We will be like enchanted children witnessing splendid processions. We will remain silent. And we will see the beauty, the wonderful, the gentle smiles of the monks.

Introduction

From Cluny, Saint-Maur, and Solesmes to Fontgombault

For fifteen hundred years, beyond the twists and turns of history, all monastic orders — be they Benedictine, Cistercian, or Trappist — and all congregations such as Cluny, Saint-Maur, or Solesmes have adhered to one fundamental principle — that is, *The Rule of Saint Benedict*:

> The monastery, it is written, if possible, must be established in such a way that one finds within it all the necessary things, such as water, a mill, a garden, a bakery, and workshops, so that various trades can be practiced within the enclosure itself, thus ensuring that the monks have

> no need to venture outside. This is not at all beneficial for their souls. We want this Rule to be frequently read in the community, so that none of the brothers can excuse themselves on the grounds of ignorance. (Chapter 66)

But to understand Fontgombault, it is first necessary to consider Solesmes and its re-founder. When he sought to restore Benedictine life in the Solesmes priory, the man who was then only the young Father Prosper Guéranger had to turn to history. At the time, in 1830, there were no longer any French monasteries of black-robed monks.* Certainly, he had been able to approach the Cistercians because the white-robed monks† from the Abbey of Notre-Dame-de-la-Trappe, known as the Grande Trappe, had returned to France during the Restoration. But a stay with Dom Antoine de Beauregard at the Abbey of Melleray had made it clear to Father Guéranger that he should not draw inspiration from this branch derived from the Benedictine trunk.

In 1790, when the National Constituent Assembly abolished the monastic orders, two major bodies gathered most of the Benedictine monasteries: the Cluny order and the Saint-Maur congregation. The former had almost nine centuries of existence and played a crucial role between the tenth and twelfth centuries in the gradual assertion of the Church's autonomy against secular power. However, by the end of the eighteenth century, it had lost some of its influence, in part due

* This expression refers to the Benedictine monks who wear the black tunic, scapular, and cowl.

† Thus the Cistercians and Trappists are called, who wear the white tunic, the black scapular, and the white cowl. The Benedictine Order was founded by Saint Benedict of Nursia in 529. Its Rule, which advocates a balance between prayer and work, achieved great success. In 817, it was imposed on all monasteries in the Carolingian Empire. Robert de Molesme (1029–1111) in 1098, and later Bernard of Clairvaux (1090–1153), sought new paths of perfection and spoke out against the supposed magnificence of Cluny. The Cistercian path emerged from this desire to renew monasticism around a more ascetic ideal. In the seventeenth century, Armand-Jean de Rancé (1626–1700) at La Trappe had the same idea and proposed a stricter adherence to the Rule.

to feudal laws of commendation,[‡] and was divided into two branches, the Reformed and the Old Observance. In contrast, the Saint-Maur congregation, established in 1618 from a reform that had originated in the Duchy of Lorraine, then statutorily attached to the Holy Roman Empire, reached its peak in the seventeenth and eighteenth centuries.

What fascinated Dom Guéranger at Cluny was not only the importance given to liturgical work but also the attachment to the Holy See. From its foundation in 910, Duke William of Aquitaine stipulated that the monastery would be subject to no earthly power, but only to the apostle Peter. Could it be possible to rediscover this golden age?

For the young priest, the priority, after the revolutionary storm, was to restore Christianity. This involved rebuilding a network of monasteries that could ensure the public prayer of the Church. At the same time, he understood that it was not a matter of living in the nineteenth century as in the days of the glorious Abbots Mayeul (910–994) or Odilon (962–1048) of Cluny. How could one maintain an office that the Cluniacs themselves had reduced over the centuries? In the eighteenth century, their liturgy had largely followed the neo-Gallican evolution, so Dom Guéranger did not consider restoring it. Furthermore, he did not want to adopt the regime of the Ordo Cluniacensis, where houses founded by the Burgundian abbey remained as priories, and abbatial authority was reserved for the superior of Cluny alone. He preferred the association of monasteries *sui juris*, each with its own abbot, united in the same congregation.

In the case of Saint-Maur, closer to his own time, the legacy seemed easier to take up. Dom Guéranger drew inspiration from the constitutions of Saint-Maur to formulate his own legislative

‡ In the system of commendation, the "commendatory abbot," whether the superior of the abbey (who often does not reside there) or a layperson, directly receives its income without possessing any spiritual authority over the monks. This system led many French monasteries into deep crises during the seventeenth and eighteenth centuries.

text. He adopted a significant portion of their ceremonies and many customs. He even wanted to revive the congregation title, but Pope Gregory XVI opposed it because in Rome the name Saint-Maur was too closely associated with Jansenism, Gallicanism, and even philosophism,* which he condemned. The Church encouraged him to go further back into the Benedictine tradition. Dom Guéranger subsequently congratulated himself on this Roman requirement and returned to the monastic concept of the Benedictines founder, Saint Benedict of Nursia (498–547), where each monastery is a family under the paternal authority of its abbot.

Furthermore, it can be read in the first legislative text of his congregation, approved by Gregory XVI after long negotiations, that "it will take the place of the ancient congregations of Cluny, Saint-Vanne and Hydulphe, and Saint-Maur, and will inherit their privileges, but cannot take their name." This is how the *Congregatio gallica*, later renamed the Congregation of Saint-Pierre de Solesmes, was born. The heritage of the ancient monastic centuries was received with careful consideration, and the new Benedictine family developed autonomously and uniquely, drawing from the source, *The Rule of Saint Benedict*, to the extent that other monastic restorations of the nineteenth century sought training and support.

When Dom Guéranger died on January 30, 1875, he was at the helm of an abbey whose influence was already established worldwide. His successors, especially Dom Paul Delatte (1848–1937), brilliantly developed his legacy.

At the refounding of Fontgombault in 1948, Solesmes and its abbot, Dom Cozien, were extremely generous. It should be noted

* Throughout the seventeenth and eighteenth centuries, the popes sought to curb movements that aimed to organize the Church autonomously from Rome. Jansenism, primarily through its doctrine on grace; Gallicanism, through its desire for political emancipation aimed at creating national churches; and Enlightenment philosophy, aiming to free humanity from religious authority, found themselves in conflict with Rome.

that at the time, Solesmes had 125 monks, and the novices, held up by the war and, for some, by captivity, had now been able to complete their studies and receive ordination. Recruitment was flourishing. Fontgombault was, therefore, the first foundation of Solesmes since their return from exile in the 1920s.†

In this context, Dom Cozien was able to send twenty monks to the lands of Berry, quickly joined by others from Solesmes. He purchased the buildings of Fontgombault from the Diocese of Bourges and authorized the necessary initial expenditures to adapt the premises to their original purpose. Many books donated by Solesmes formed a valuable collection for the library.

Finally, Dom Cozien appointed Dom Édouard Roux, then the novice master at Solesmes and highly esteemed by the community, as the superior, leaning heavily on him.

With Dom Roux's appointment as abbot in 1953 and the establishment of the priory as an abbey, the young foundation on the banks of the Creuse River quickly gained its independence. The abbey then flourished and prospered.

Now, let us enter Fontgombault!

† After the Law on Associations, the Benedictines of Solesmes left their monastery in September 1901 for England. They settled on the Isle of Wight, where they founded Quarr Abbey. They returned to the banks of the Sarthe River in 1922.

I
First Visit to the Monastic City

Dom Prior had asked me to wait for him at the entrance to the enclosure, and as usual he was on time. He had just finished leading a class on chant. After a few words, we passed through the wooden door that separates the world of men from that of the monks to enter the cloister.

At Fontgombault, the cloister is relatively austere. This impression is certainly due to the large windows that separate it from the inner garden. During winter the severity of the climate and humidity often keep them closed. The beautiful, exposed white stones, ochre flooring, and delicate arches might mitigate this simplicity, but the severity remains. In summer, the monks open the doors wide to let the warmth inside, and the long corridors become more cheerful.

We admired the four classically designed flower beds in the center of the cloister. At the time of my visit the small square enclosures had become wild and rustic. Gaillardias, columbines, summer chrysanthemums, Californian poppies with their abundant orange flowers, marigolds, four o'clock flowers, wild roses, geraniums, and lavender bushes grew in the joyful chaos of a new English garden. In the center, an unassuming cross stood. Rows of boxwood formed the boundaries of this unconventional tableau. Some monks did not hide their nostalgia for the beautiful rigor of the old rose beds maintained by Father Abbot Antoine.

A wild duck had discovered the advantageous nature of this cloistered universe. She regularly made her nest in the colorful tangle. The bird was not well-versed in the Benedictine rigor of the place. A few days after their birth, the monks gently led the ducklings to the banks of the Creuse.

My attention was drawn to the tower, shaped like a keep, that overlooked the church. The original tower, more slender, had collapsed in a fire. In the seventeenth century, they rebuilt this square bell tower, and subsequent generations never took the time to add architectural features that would have given it a semblance of elegance.

Near a reproduction of a fifteenth-century Pietà, nestled in the *armarium* ("ambry"), the passage from the cloister to the southern part of the transept was grandiose. The high steps leading to the abbey church invariably conveyed a sense of spiritual elevation. Reduced to ruins in 1569 by the Calvinists, the nave remained a heap of rubble for a long time where vegetation took root. Nevertheless, it retained its soul. Restored by Father Abbot Lenoir, a priest from the Diocese of Bourges, at the end of the nineteenth century, it was constructed using material from nearby Poitou quarries. Its encrusted whiteness contrasted with the patina of the ancient sections, where the walls of the surviving Romanesque era impressed with the austerity of their unadorned openings.

The central nave, its peaceful arrangement, the intense light of summer afternoons, the perspective toward the distant and mysterious sanctuary, cannot fail to move visitors.

At the end of the main aisle, the funerary slab of Pierre de l'Étoile, the founder of the abbey who died in 1114, forms a symbolic divide between the public area and the church's sanctuary. The master had been buried in the old chapter room of the monastery, under the threshold of the door leading to the cloister. His remains were transferred in 1954. He is represented in monk's attire, holding a crosier in one hand and *The Rule of Saint Benedict* in the other, with a monastic tonsure. An epitaph engraved in uncials says: "*Petrus eram dictus, nunc sum sine nomine pulvis; sed miserante Deo de pulvere credo resurgam. Dic homo qui transit Deo ut mihi propicietur. Nunc quod es ipse fui ; quod sum modo tu quoque fies.*" ("They called me Peter, now I am nameless dust; but, by God's mercy, I believe I will rise from the dust. Ask, O man who passes by, that God be merciful to me. What you are now, I once was; what I am now, you will become.")

In front of the tomb, the choir dimensions reveal the remarkable confidence of the architect, who did not hesitate to raise the vault nearly seventeen meters high. With its unobstructed forms, elegance, and harmonious layout, the sanctuary of Fontgombault ranks among the most accomplished of Romanesque compositions. In the apse, six cylindrical columns resting on a low wall support seven slender arches, allowing ample light to flood in through the large windows of the ambulatory.

How can we characterize the ambitious project of the builders of Fontgombault? The twelfth-century monks aimed to construct a building whose grandeur would have impressed the austere Saint Bernard. They used the most advanced techniques to enhance the lighting of the church. This trend, notable in the church of Cluny, built by Saint Hugh, is also found in Berry. It ultimately led to the luminous walls of Gothic architecture, whose prototype can be recognized in the choir of Saint-Denis, the kings' necropolis consecrated by Abbot Suger in 1144, just a few years after Fontgombault's dedication.

However, it must be believed that the criticism by the abbot of Clairvaux, condemning the use of apotropaic monster sculptures in monastic churches as distractions for the monks, was heeded on the banks of the Creuse. The same spirit guided these monks, who sought a return to greater simplicity. In the context of the new monasticism, Fontgombault falls midway between the Cistercian demands, which focused on the perfection of lines and volumes, and the richness of the buildings of the Fontevraud order.

I continued my journey with Dom Prior. Just outside the church, an array of ancient rooms opens onto French-style gardens. We first entered a rather narrow room that the monks call the small sacristy. It dates to the fifteenth century, and its rib-vaulted ceiling is quite elegant. On one of the ribs, I noticed an abbatial coat of arms; although the Revolution of 1793 had chiseled away several stones, one could still discern the crosier with a keen eye. Near the wall is a massive dark wood chasuble chest, a masterpiece of sacred art. The furniture had been designed to fit the exact proportions of the room. Commissioned by Dom Andrieu, the restorer of the abbey in the late seventeenth century, it was sold at the beginning of the revolutionary turmoil. In the 1960s, the monks found it in a farmhouse and embarked on a meticulous restoration. Small labels on the marquetry drawers indicate where the monks can store their liturgical linen: D. Hebdomadarius, D. Prior, Rmus D. D. Antonius, D. Subprior. Reliquaries placed at both ends enhanced the dignity of the whole room. Nearby, a beautiful portrait of Pope Francis was simply hung on the wall.

Once through a beautiful door and a few more steps, we entered the large sacristy, restored at the beginning of the eighteenth century thanks to the vicar general of the Diocese of Bourges. The former monk received emoluments in this role. In the early days of the abbey, this room served as the chapter hall where the Benedictines buried their abbots. Later, during the second half of the nineteenth century, when the Trappists oversaw the abbey, they decided to divide it into two parts, dedicating one solely to their chapter. As time passes, each era corresponds to a different use of the space. At the heart of this palimpsest, a Latin inscription poetically concludes the history: "*Hoc in antiquo capitulo abbates fratres et benefactores non pauci in spe resurrectionis quiescent.*" ("In this ancient chapter, many abbots, brothers, and benefactors rest in the hope of resurrection."). A few meters away, the tombstone of a twelfth-century knight, a contemporary of Pierre de l'Étoile, serves as a poignant symbol of time suspended in this small land of Fontgombault.

A relatively recent chasuble chest occupied the center of the room. The seventeenth-century ivory-carved Christ on the wall, Dom Pateau's evangeliary, a sublime work created using medieval techniques, and the Byzantine-style enamel processional cross crafted by the abbey's subprior all displayed a timeless commitment to beauty. On that day, chasubles were neatly folded on every piece of furniture in both rooms, delicately prepared for the next day's Mass.

Not far from there, I entered the current chapter room, which seemed timeless to me. The damp walls called for restoration. The room was divided in the middle by rather ugly columns. At the back stood the neo-Gothic cathedra of Father Abbot, topped with his coat of arms, which exhibited no ostentation. On the coat of arms, I read, "De gueules au rai d'escarboucle d'or, fleurdelysé et pommeté, allumé d'azur." Its red color harkened to that of warriors. In front, small stools were perfectly aligned, where the monks gathered every morning after prime. They listened to the martyrology, the holy *Rule*, and prayed for the deceased. In the evening, before compline, the monks returned for spiritual reading. This was where the abbot's conferences to the community took place once a week, as well as chapter meetings for canonical matters. On the walls, the monks had hung portraits of the great dignitaries of the abbeys of Solesmes and Fontgombault: Dom Philippe Dupont, the titular abbot; Dom Prosper Guéranger, the venerated founder; Dom Paul Delatte, the intellectual; Dom Germain Cozien, the builder; Mother Cécile Bruyère, the mystic; Dom Édouard Roux, the first abbot of Fontgombault after the return of the Benedictines; and Dom Jean Roy, who passed away in a state of sanctity. Their presence was reassuring.

The Rule of Saint Benedict, bound to commemorate Dom Forgeot's twenty-fifth anniversary of profession, was placed on a large lectern. At the other end, a beautiful statue venerated as Our Lady of the Grottoes sat on an unremarkable piece of furniture. Its history was astonishing: the Virgin and Child belonged to the monks, but during the Revolution the villagers secretly reclaimed it at the time of the monastery's sale as national property. They feared that the Blessed Lady might be destroyed. It was hidden in a cave on the banks of the Creuse, then passed down through generations of families. As soon as the monks of Solesmes returned, the endearing statue made its way back to the abbey. Today, the wooden statue is carried in procession for the feasts of August 15, the Assumption and December 8, the Immaculate Conception.

The representation of the mother of Jesus was flanked by two small altars, one dedicated to Joan of Arc, surmounted by a portrait of Pope Francis, and the other to Saint Thérèse. The latter was crafted by a monk who was a carpenter at the abbey. The subprior fashioned the gilded copper cross and Byzantine-style candlesticks that adorned it, as well as the metal bas-relief made from exorcised and melted satanic idols. On this morning, a lay brother* had placed an elegant arrangement of white roses and yellow dahlias at Mary's feet.

* In monastic orders, the lay brothers, or *conversi*, are primarily responsible for manual labor and the secular affairs of the abbey, in contrast to the fathers, who dedicate themselves to the *opus dei* (the "work of God") and to study.

We then proceeded through a passageway, an old and somewhat dilapidated corridor. The long room where the Benedictine monks store their ample choir robes demonstrated the monks' renunciation of material possessions just a few meters away. Death notices were displayed on a board humorously referred to as the "babillard," meaning chatterbox, by the monks. Here, they could read prayer intentions and practical information.

Adjacent to it, in a small scriptorium, the brothers used to display birth announcements, marriage notices, ordination announcements, profession notices, postcards, and handwritten letters received from all over the world. A letter from Dom Pateau during an absence began with these delicate lines: "Very dear Reverend Father abbot Antoine, dear Father Prior, very dear children."

On the wall, two poorly crafted portraits of the Trappist abbots from the nineteenth century, Dom Albéric and Dom Dosithée, hung alongside a picture of Abbot Lenoir, who repurchased the monastery after the expulsions in 1903. A group photo of the monks, taken in 1975, completed the decor. I admired the beautiful simplicity that the monks maintained in these spaces.

On the floor, pieces of capitals, column bases, some stones from the church's portal, an altar table, and a keystone formed a strange antiquities museum. These relics from the Middle Ages, scattered without a clear order, were witnesses to the glorious history of Fontgombault. And near an old piece of furniture, under yellowed plastic, sat a 1950s typewriter — the monks cared little about the passing of time. Here, the community consulted a few newspapers to stay informed about current events.

We then passed through the flower room, a multipurpose space where the monks arranged their bouquets, and reached the library adjacent to the large scriptorium. I could hear the sound of water from the monks' power-plant dam. Books were neatly arranged on sturdy, oversized tables. The most prominent piece of furniture displayed a taxidermied fox with beautiful red fur sitting proudly. A plaque near its delicate paws read, "Homeric battle Inuk — large fox, December 10, 2018."

Inuk was a six-year-old German shepherd, adored by his master, a monk-farmer, but not held in high regard by the abbot. The dog had proven to be fast and meticulous. That winter, the fox had been lured by the enticing scent of the chicken coop. The audacious fox even took refuge in the barn, where it made itself at home for a few days. Exhausted, Inuk finally discovered it. However, the fox was perched high, out of reach, and the dog jumped in vain while the fox taunted him. Brother Raphael-Marie, drawn by the commotion, found the scene. He installed a small ledge for the dog to reach the fox's hideout. Inuk grabbed the enemy by the throat. The fox's final hour had arrived.

Facing Inuk's adversary was a portrait of the Blessed Emperor Charles of Austria, the husband of Zita, a friend of the Solesmes Abbey, alongside those of Popes Benedict XVI and John Paul II. Perched on a pillar, a stuffed woodpecker and owl looked down, slightly mocking, at a *Petite vie de Agnès de Langeac* and the complete works of Catherine of Siena. The monks had a sense of Baroque decoration.

Finally, we entered the library, which housed more than seventy thousand volumes. It was the well-defended domain of the novice master. Dom Jean meticulously managed this imposing, dimly lit room. A wooden board indicated the layout of the shelves with notarial precision. Each book was cataloged and had a machine-typed index card. The monks would fill out a borrowing and return slip. In essence, I realized that Fontgombault's library operated just like its older counterparts from the 1950s.

However, a small curiosity transported us much further back than the postwar years. According to an ancient monastic tradition, behind the "hell" grate, in a dusty corner of the room, the monks kept a first edition by Voltaire at a safe distance. The philosopher shared the space with books that had been indexed.

Fontgombault's library also held valuable incunabula, which were carefully stored in a safe. But the monks were tight-lipped about them so as not to arouse covetousness. The cellarer didn't say a word about it. He wanted to continue to sleep soundly on both ears.

After the communal rooms, it was time to explore the abbey's attics, barns, and workshops. Fontgombault is a small island. The monks live far from the world and provide for a good part of their material needs themselves. Dom Prior showed me the workshop that handled the monastery's printing and binding activities. The printers, large hammers for flattening, pots of glue, and the sewing machine gave the impression of an ancient and noble shop straight out of a nineteenth-century industrial novel. Nearby there was the laundry, on the banks of the Creuse; the astonishing power plant; the shoemaking shop, which produced sandals, shoes, and belts; the stonemasonry and the paraments workshop for making monastic clothing; the pottery, where jars and amphorae were meticulously arranged on shelves around large kilns; and, finally, the forges that would make even the most meticulous general quartermasters envious.

This wide-ranging tableau was nothing without the agricultural and food activities of the monastery. The immense kitchen, the bakery, the apiary, the cellar, the vegetable garden, the pantry with its hundreds of jars of preserves, the incredible orchards, the rows of apple and pear trees that descended to the foot of the monks' cemetery, the gardens, the greenhouses, the model farm (that produced milk, cheese, eggs, veal, cows, pigs, fodder, and grains) all resembled a perfect world.

If Fontgombault could speak, what would it say to the secular world? In a clear and confident voice, it would dare to assert:

I am the unyielding citadel. I am the abbey of Pierre de l'Étoile, built on the rock of the high Creuse. I am the one who will endure for a long time. I am the faithful, beautiful, and misunderstood house of prayer. But make no mistake. None of this matters. On this earth, the monk is attached to nothing. He is passing through. Only God matters.

II
Things Seen, Things Heard in the Abbey

Sunday, June 16, 2019, the melancholy
On the Office of Compline

After dinner, the retreatants were still wandering on the lawn that opened onto the park. The linden trees saturated the air with their powerful scent. The abbey was quiet, and I could hear the distant song of birds. The time for the last service of the day was approaching, the time for compline, which is the final liturgical prayer of the hours.

An elderly father was praying, his body bent over near a wall in the ambulatory. I had the impression that he had remained motionless for centuries. The silence was pure, and the soft summer light invited daydreaming. In the long nave, the guests and the faithful were gradually returning. The stones seemed to long for the monks.

A young brother came to open the cloister door that led to the choir. Then another one entered to ring the bells. The grand procession began, inaugurated by the two abbots. From the cloister, the line of monks, arranged in pairs, stretched slowly. All the monks had pulled their hoods over their heads. They took them off as they entered the church before bowing before the altar. After a perfectly executed, almost choreographed reverence, they entered the wooden stalls.

At the delicate sound of a mallet, the hebdomadary monk began the *Confiteor* alone, repeated a second time by the community, with heads and bodies bowed. Every evening, the prayer is the same, the ritual unchanging.

The chant of the psalms began. The rhythm was clear, simple, so precise that one could lose one's breath listening. After Psalm 133, the words of the traditional hymn for compline, which I knew well, never failed to move me:

Te lucis ante terminum
Rerum Creator, poscimus,
Ut solita clementia
Sis praesul ad custodiam.
Procul recedant somnia
Et noctium phantasmata
Hostemque nostrum comprime,
Ne polluantur corpora.

Before the end of the day,
We beseech you, Creator of all,
In your customary clemency,
To watch over us and protect us.
Banish far away our dreams

And the phantoms of the night,
And restrain our enemy,
So that our bodies remain undefiled.

The voices were deep, the vaults motionless, frozen by an ageless beauty. And the texts continued. The beautiful invocation that asked God for restful sleep and protection from nightmares was like the grandiose sunsets that gradually disappear on the horizon; the last notes faded away, never to return. At twenty minutes to nine, the day was ending.

Everyone knew the final moments of the service. At the entrance of the sanctuary, a monk would come to light two candles placed under a statue of the Virgin Mary. Then, Father Abbot would bless the entire community. The majestic chant of the *Salve Regina* would resound. It came from the depths of the Church's history. The piece could bring tears of joy and melancholy.

Finally, the abbot would sprinkle each of the monks with holy water. His steps would echo on the old wooden floor. Kneeling, each one would bow as he passed by: "*Asperges me, Domine, hyssopo, et mundabor: lavabis me, et super nivem dealbabor.*" ("You will sprinkle me, O Lord, with hyssop, and I shall be cleansed; you will wash me, and I shall be whiter than snow.")

One detail stood out in the gradually darkening church. Amid the monks, a postulant in civilian clothing contrasted with the impressive black mass. Immobile monks stood before the long cords that seemed to descend from heaven. The bells sounded three sets of three chimes and then rang out. At the signal of the same mallet, the monks dispersed freely to pray to Our Lady of a Good Death. In an instant, they could be seen kneeling around the church. They commended themselves to Mary one last time. That evening, five young children in shorts from a local family, hands folded, accompanied them.

The prior headed toward the back of the church to pray before the icon of Divine Mercy. He knelt at the foot of the statue of Our Lady, prayed again, and disappeared into the shadow of the enclosure.

In the choir, Dom Forgeot walked slowly. Then he knelt, too, near the tomb of his illustrious predecessor, Dom Jean Roy, buried next to the tabernacle. On the slightly polished white stone, there was a simple inscription: *Ioannes Abbas — 1921–1977.*

Thursday, June 20, 2019
Corpus Christi

The weather was gloomy. The day before, as the wind blew, I had seen the monks trimming the hedges near the wall that bordered the orchard. After breakfast, the monastery had become a beehive: the monks were busy preparing for Corpus Christi. A small group of them worked diligently to spread rose petals on the square. The brothers were well versed in the task, repeated diligently and eagerly every year.

They used large wooden frames to create harmonious patterns. Hundreds of dried flowers or small tinted wood chips were used to form scrolls and geometric figures on the ground, including hearts, fleur-de-lis, stars, and rudimentary waves.

In the middle of the meadow, other monks were setting up a platform. This task was more physical. They hammered, pushed, and adjusted. Then the monks placed a gigantic anchor topped with a white cross on it. They had laid carpets at the foot of this temporary altar. At the front of the platform, a path of branches, scattered with wildflowers, and in its center a cloud of rose petals completed this childlike scenery.

Were we in 1969 or 2019? An old monastery van made back-and-forth trips to deliver equipment, an elderly man took photos, a monk hurried to the farm on a bicycle, and the prior oversaw the operations with meticulous focus while organ notes emanated distinctly from the abbey — rehearsal of the musical pieces for the day.

Inside, the choir and the ambulatory radiated the unique majesty of ancient stones that had nothing left to prove. A few monks crossed the transept quickly. One of them placed liturgical items on the small sanctuary wall. Another brought stacks of large books for guests. A brother in the kitchen had donned a white alb. He came to light the tall candelabra on the high altar, adorned with yellow hybrid tea roses.

Distant echoes in the nave, soft and measured footsteps, barely perceptible murmurs: The high Mass was being prepared. But silence always enveloped these small sounds. Between the choir stalls and the altar, a dark wooden throne, neo-Gothic in style, surrounded by three small seats on large Persian rugs, signified the solemnity of the day.

At 10:15 in the morning, four monks arrived to ring the bells. They rang loudly, announcing the start of Mass. Then the music of the final peals faded, and silence returned.

At 10:30, precisely at the start of a huge bell ringing, a procession of monks dressed in perfectly pressed albs over their black habits entered the choir. As they entered, the grand organ resounded. Father Abbot, preceded by eighteen assistants, led the way. His red and gold damask garments made a strong impression.

Then he ascended to the throne. Three monks around him had lifted their hoods, and three novices sat on the floor at his feet. One held the miter in his liturgical scarf, and another carried the crosier. They resembled the apostles gathered around Christ, absorbed in deep and gentle prayer.

A brother had come to present a censer. Later, with an acolyte, they would spare no effort. The two monks would make wonderful spirals of incense rise in great billows.

In a distant chapel, I saw four elderly monks reciting the

psalms in a low voice. They looked tired, white-haired, and hunched. At the end of terce, Father Abbot changed his liturgical vestments while remaining in place; he took off his cope and put on a chasuble. The Mass began.

The abbot incensed the high altar. He circled it, then returned to the throne as the choir sang a slow and smooth *Kyrie*. The apostles' scene around the abbot, a striking image worthy of a great painter, reformed. A brother held the miter, another continued to carry the crosier. People rose at the sound of the *Gloria* and immediately sat down. The angelic chant continued with rare dignity. I looked at the prior. He bowed his head so deeply, covered by his hood, lost in unfathomable prayer, that I could believe he had breathed his last. That's when the strangely crystalline, almost unique, voice of the epistle reader transported the soul. Gregorian notes rose again, and the *Alleluia* reached the sublime.

The red and blue light piercing through the stained glass was delicate. The abbey had left its century; we were in unfathomable communion with the Benedictine monks of the past, those of Cluny, those of Saint-Maur, and those of Solesmes. After the song of the Gospel, the abbot began his homily by quoting Paul VI. I remember a beautiful phrase: "Let us place the act of heaven upon the earth." After the Creed, which the monks executed unusually slowly, a magnificent piece echoed from the organ.

Golden light flooded the sanctuary during the canon. It was dazzling. The congregation prayed intensely. I couldn't imagine a more perfect liturgical setting.

Benedicamus Domino ("Let us bless the Lord"). Father Abbot had donned a magnificent chasuble to begin the procession, holding in his hands a gigantic monstrance containing the holy Sacrament, protected by the ombrellino (a canopy held over the Eucharist during processions). In front of him, the monks advanced, carrying candles. A thick cloud of incense rose throughout the church. The moment was grand, terribly poetic. At the abbey exit, on the square, monks surrounded Father Abbot, holding up a large rectangular canopy.

The monks sang the hymn *Pange, lingua, gloriosi.* They walked toward the wooden altar in the middle of the meadow, stepping on the carpet of wildflowers scattered on the ground. Father Abbot had a focused and solemn expression. I saw Dom Forgeot following the verses in his chant book with the same dedication as a young novice experiencing the feast of Corpus Christi for the first time. The monks formed a semicircle around the altar, kneeling in the green grass of early summer. Around them, the crowd of faithful imitated them. Doves cooed, the farm's rooster crowed in rapid succession, and the wind rustled through the linden trees. The scene was perfect, delightfully outdated, without a tasteless detail.

After this, the monks returned to the church. For the Benediction with the Eucharist, they sang the *Tantum ergo.* From the back of the church, the large eagle on the choir's lectern seemed surrounded by extraordinary points of light. The two seven-branched candelabras on the high altar heightened these impressions.

Then the solemn procession withdrew. The feeling of fulfillment that can envelop the heart in these moments of grace is rare.

At the exit, I crossed paths with the man who had been at the guesthouse. He was hitchhiking back home with his backpack to the small town of Blanc, about ten kilometers away, to catch a bus.

Monday, June 24, 2019, Solemn Mass
The Nativity of Saint John the Baptist

In the missal used for this Mass, it was written:

> "Among those born of women there is no one greater than John the Baptist," Our Lord said. He is greater than Elijah, Isaiah, Jeremiah, and Malachi; he is the Prophet par excellence, to the point of being nothing more than a "Voice" of God. But Our Lord also said, he is even more than a prophet: he is the immediate "Precursor" of Christ; he is the one of whom it is written: "Behold, I send my messenger ahead of you, who will prepare your way."

The discourse was magnificent. It urged prayer, humility, and self-abasement.

However, a few days after Corpus Christi, I felt like I was coming to contemplate the same painting in an unchanged museum. On the canvas the same throne, the same fabrics, the same faces, the same arrangement in service of God's glory.

Father Abbot was present in the fullest sense of the term: He watched over his sons. He exuded serenity, simplicity, and joy. Incense wafted up during the *Gloria*, and the light pierced through the stained-glass windows. Religious silence, sacred words, and Gregorian notes intertwined endlessly. This was the eternal order of Mass at Fontgombault.

The repetition of liturgical gestures is perhaps, simply, the repetition of the same love. Everything began anew. The processions, the pomp, the mystery. A day, a year, a century ago, a devotee experienced the same feelings.

I remembered the words of Dom Forgeot. From a monastic life, a monk retains almost nothing in memory. They remember date of entry, the profession, the day of ordination for priests, and a few events, happy or sad. The rest evaporates in these extraordinary ceremonies where the heart pours out, and the soul soars.

The choir sang a *Hallelujah* of such depth that it could bring tears. In a very dense homily, without losing a true lightness, Father Abbot spoke of guardian angels and patron saints. He said quite seriously:

> Contemplating the saints of heaven might lead us to compare them. Some Scriptures seem to incline in that direction, like this affirmation from the Lord: "Among those born of women there has arisen no one greater than John the Baptist" (Mt 11:11). Let us be certain, however, that the saints of heaven do not compete. They are in the light of God and sing his praises.

He concluded with a more solemn tone:

> John the Baptist was named "the monk of the New Testament." The monks of today still wish to follow in his footsteps. Through the witness of their life in the desert, through their daily fidelity to the harsh and arduous path they have freely chosen in response to God's call, they want to invite the people of their time to embark on the desert path, to commit themselves to the path of God. Even though two millennia separate us from John, it is the same witness that we must deliver, asking us poor sinners to follow the example of the saintly precursor: In the face of a deceitful world, ignorant of God and his laws, to recall the absolute of God, of his truth, to walk "before him in the spirit ... to turn the hearts of the fathers to the children, / and the disobedient to the wisdom of the just, / to make ready for the Lord a people prepared" (Lk 1:17).

And the Mass continued, carried by its pearls of wisdom.

I observed the stark seriousness of the prior. He descended to the stalls to offer the sign of peace. Each brother then turned to his neighbor to embrace them. During Communion, Father

Bernard gently gathered the guests near the sanctuary and directed them toward the nave. After Mass, children, young people, couples, grandparents lingered before the statue of Our Lady of a Good Death. As usual.

Tuesday, June 25, 2019
Silence of the morning Masses

It was 6:30 in the morning. In the stalls, the monks were finishing lauds. The second office of the monastic day welcomes the sunrise, symbolizing the resurrection of Christ. More than others, it is a prayer of joy, thanksgiving, and jubilation. Every day, the monks recite the last three texts of the Psalter. Two of them begin with the supplication "*Laudate Dominum*" ("Praise the Lord"). They gave their name to this office and are reminiscent of St. Francis of Assisi's beautiful Canticle of the Creatures:

> Praise the Lord, you who are in the heavens...
> Praise him, all you angels...
> Sun and moon, praise him: stars and light, praise him all together...
> Praise the Lord, you who are on the earth ... fire, hail, snow, ice...
> You mountains, and all hills...
> Wild animals and all livestock. (see Psalm 148)

Then, for the first Angelus prayer of that summer day, the monks knelt. In the abbey, the altars were ready. The brothers lit the two candles placed at the end of each. Around the ambulatory and near the pillars of the great nave, the rough stone altars welcomed about twenty monks. The moment that was beginning was of unparalleled power and grandeur.

A small number of early morning faithful, freshly awakened,

were praying. At 6:40, the priests arrived together. They came out of the sacristy, carrying their chalices in their hands, hoods raised, preceded by lay brothers and a few altar boys.

The sacred gestures reminded me of the old photographic negatives. They were both similar and different at the same time. The whispered words, the tones of the chalices, the folds of the chasubles, each sound became more extraordinary. I recognized the guestmaster, the porter, the cellarer, and the infirmarian. A faithful person coughed, and only we heard him. Outside, the concert of birdsong seemed never-ending. Through these chirps, God added a final touch to his sublime tableau.

The altar boys moved the lectern with the Missal placed on it. The low Masses were said quickly; they were microscopic mirrors of heaven. If perfection could exist on this earth, it would resemble these pure, charming, and humble Masses.

Around 6:55, the priests began reciting the canon. I watched in amazement as these gestures repeated with a slight delay from one altar to another. The hosts were consecrated. The moment of elevation arrived. Then the wine was turned into blood. The faithful knelt on the rustic benches near the altars to receive Communion. In the axial chapel at the back of the church, three monks did the same. They did not move; they were no longer of this world.

One priest returned to the sacristy, then another, a third, and all the others. They walked with their heads bowed, as they had arrived, hoods raised, preceded by the brothers and some sleepy young servers.

I looked at my watch. It was 7:10. The low Masses were finished. The brothers had meticulously extinguished the candles. Three or four of the most devout faithful were still praying a little.

Today, it would be hot. A heatwave was forecasted for Fontgombault. For a few monks, another task began: the time for thanksgiving while walking in the cloister.

Outside, on Departmental Road 950, which ran alongside the abbey, crossing the village from one end to the other, the children's bus from the countryside sped toward the Collège du Blanc.

Wednesday, August 7, 2019
Starry night

The bells rang in the night. It was five o'clock in the morning. As I crossed the long corridor on the first floor, I heard the sound of rain, then discovered downstairs that the door to the guesthouse was slightly ajar. The sky was black. The tall trees in the park were no longer distinguishable, shrouded in a light fog.

A great mantle of silence hung in the abbey. Some monks were already praying. One knelt before Our Lady of a Good Death, another walked with bowed head in the ambulatory, while the farmer monk prayed in a transept arm.

A soft and maternal twilight enveloped the monks' steps. At the matins office, there was no procession. Each freely joined their choir stall. At 5:15 a.m., the office began. Dom Jean gave the traditional mallet tap.

In a monastery, the bell and the hammer govern the etiquette. The hammer also serves the refectory and the chapter. Symbolizing regularity and observance, the hammer is the superior's instrument to enforce order and peace. The bell is a sacramental; it is the voice of the Lord calling to prayer and warding off demons.

The Gregorian chant of the night seemed to me to be of infinite slowness. Liturgists speak of a recitation *recto tono*: the text is sung on the same note from start to finish. The music reflects the monks' inner peace.

On that August day, matins was organized around two nocturnes, each composed of six psalms. After Psalm 3, called "of expectation," which allows the latecomers to join the church, the invitatory opened the praise with Psalm 94, and then the first nocturne began.

In the midst of matins, between the two nocturnes, a voice resonated. A monk recited from memory a brief lesson taken that night from the Book of Wisdom. The abbey seemed frozen. Delicate lamps illuminated the upper parts of the abbey. The voices responded to each other. The monks were like angels engaged in a gentle choral combat. The slow chant never ceased. The abbey gently rolled on the waves, and Father Abbot held the helm.

The Berry Benedictines stood up, prostrated, sat down, and knelt like little automatons who knew everything that God expected of them while the world slept.

I shuddered at the thought of matins in the icy cold of winter. For the moment, the temperature was delightful. The heat had penetrated the thick walls, and nothing could disturb the gentle serenity of the fathers.

Looking around, I thought that one or two monks must still be in the arms of Morpheus.

At 5:40, a brother stealthily brought the liturgical objects for a low Mass. At the same time, an elderly monk emerged from the sacristy. The slightly hunched man walked with a cane. He disappeared into the ambulatory dimness. He seemed to have come from the depths of ages. I didn't see him again.

The monks continued their uninterrupted communion with God. No one could interrupt this long conversation. At 5:50 in the morning, they had so much to say to each other. The minutes passed like grains in an hourglass.

I struggled to conceive of Dom Forgeot's absence. Matins had become too tiring an exercise for him now. The night, deprived of even a single star, was no longer quite the same. Six o'clock had just chimed. The monks continued to sing.

In a few moments, lauds would begin. The brothers would join the fathers in the choir. "It's crowded today," a little child might have said, looking at the community at night. The monastic family of Fontgombault is complete. It is united, happy, and bound together.

Suddenly, the organ resounded. The mellifluous notes welcomed the imminent day. The Gregorian chant resumed its solemn course. It was a new birth, the announcement of a promise in the sight of God.

Lauds began with Psalm 66. Then, the monks sang Psalm 50, two other psalms, an Old Testament canticle, and then Psalms 148, 149, and 150. This order had been established by Saint Benedict in the *Rule*.

The first dawn rays gently entered the abbey. The mysterious black points of the stained-glass windows gradually illuminated. Thus the monks patiently awaited the Light of the World. They prayed for those of us who were still sleeping, who slept too much.

At 6:15, the sound of a vigorous rain shower could be heard trickling down the walls. The noise of the drops blended with the organ and the monks' chanting. A fresh breeze swept through the ambulatory. It came from the doors open to the cloister. The water brought strength and consolation to nature, which had long awaited this blessed moment.

Matins and lauds are like a slowly burning candle. The colors of the stained glass revealed themselves; the blues and reds had a miraculous depth. At 6:30, in the cloister, light had replaced the shadow. In the distance, I glimpsed Dom Forgeot. He walked with measured steps, small and gentle. A sublime image of an end, of a faithful life.

The chant was gentle, the tones firmer; majesty was settling in.

During the *Benedictus*, the Canticle of Zechariah, the bell tolled twenty-five times, announcing the *De Beata* Mass, offered every day by the abbey for the intentions of Our Lady, following a Cluniac tradition. Dom Pateau intoned the *Kyrie*, and then the *Pater Noster*.

The brothers began to prepare the altars. One of them entered in a white alb, and the sacristan made his way to the back of the church to open the doors. The monks recited the Angelus, and the bells rang loudly. The monks put away their books. It was 6:40 in the morning: the low Masses could begin.

The matins and lauds of August 7, 2019, resembled those of August 6, and August 8 would not be much different. August 9, 2020, August 10, 2021, it would be the same. Everything was similar, everything was unique.

Friday, November 8, 2019
Matins on feast of Saint Ursinus

At five in the morning, the small bell rang. This autumn, the temperature in the abbey was neither cold nor warm. All the monks were kneeling. At the moment of the first prayer, they raised their hoods.

The chant was slow. Strangely slow. How can one not fall asleep again while embarking on such a calm sea? Suddenly, a voice rose alone in the choir, and several responded to it. The supplication seemed infinite to me. Nothing better expresses the permanence of the monks' prayer than matins.

I thought of the loud noises, the strange chaos, the futile commotions, the restless hearts, the devastating passions, the repeated misfortunes outside the protective walls of the abbey.

I remembered a debate with Dom Prior about chanting. I told him that the *recto tono* chant is the shadow of sound, the musical night. In these moments, Gregorian chant perfectly expresses the monk's solitary quest. In the world, the night is a time for rest, celebration, and the unusual. Matins is the inverted world, a time for prayer, silence, and mystery. The American Trappist Thomas Merton curiously titled one of his books in French *La Nuit privée d'étoiles.* Under the moon and stars, the monks are close to God.

How many times have the monks of Fontgombault risen in the night to celebrate the matins of Saint Ursinus? As usual, the office resembled a small, rigorously codified play. Each monk held his book in the same way. The monk does not get discouraged: sitting, standing, prostrating, with a hood, without a hood, kneeling, head bowed over his book, gaze turned toward the high altar; he knows his role.

In the broad stall, the abbot's solitude was fascinating and unsettling. He always appeared to me as the captain of a ship on the high seas. At the forefront, he gives orders, maintains watches, commands, and battles. He loves his troops, and his troops love him.

The world sleeps: The monks pray for the world; men do not respond. The reality is striking, tragic, sublime.

Suddenly, a monk sneezed loudly, breaking the beautiful silence. Another one plunged into a huge white cotton cloth. And he, too, broke the silence. Another one coughed like an old tractor struggling to start. The scene seemed to last an eternity. In autumn, the abbey is damp. The monk prays to heaven, but his poor body remains on earth! Yet matins with three nocturnes are incredibly long. The matins and lauds prayer lasts nearly two hours. God is with his best workers.

In the nave, I knew that a young country priest from Brittany and a former novice were attending the office. I was sure that the monks were praying for this young man who was about to leave them.

A brother arrived. He walked along the sanctuary, went to

the apse, and knelt before the altar. He remained in prayer for so long, perfectly motionless, that I could believe he had passed from life to death. In these moments of reflection, I had already surprised myself worrying about a monk whom I discovered was strangely immobile.

A postulant who still wore civilian clothes came to prepare the altar in a side chapel. It was 5:30 in the morning. He returned obediently to the sacristy. Perhaps one day he would make his perpetual vows and become a lay brother.

In the abbey, the shadows of the columns, the faint light, made the volumes seem disproportionately large. At six o'clock, an elderly monk walked past before sinking into the darkness. Pale, ghostly, he walked with difficulty. In the distance, I heard gusts rising. The wind had entered the cloister. From my vantage point, the choir chant and the breath of the storm mingled sumptuously.

As usual, the brothers had not come to matins. They arrived one by one for the *Te Deum* chant. Before going up to the choir through the side aisle, they crossed themselves, knelt, and prayed for a long time.

I spotted Brother Jérôme-Marie, whom I had met the previous day in the garden. He was tall, serious, and wide awake.

At five minutes past six, all the brothers returned to their choir stalls. The community was gathered, young and old, those just beginning, and those approaching their final days, whenever heaven willed it. The organ resounded. The notes of a delightful melody danced in the fading night. Music is beautiful, yet its primary purpose is not artistic. It accompanies prayer. In that sense, it is radically different.

The night was no longer night. It had become a weightless time, lulled by gentle voices. The organ made the singing easier, broader, more expansive. The first cantor rose among his brothers and uttered the first words of the psalms. His warm, deep bass voice, harmoniously complete, filled the space. From a distance, I could discern his generous and noble demeanor, almost carefree. Saint Ursinus was honorably celebrated. The first Bourges bishop could be proud of the monks from his ancient diocese in Berry.

Around half past six, the monks were still standing, singing in the night. The organ continued its gentle procession. Finally, the bells rang twenty-five times during the *Benedictus*, then the Angelus at the end of lauds. And the bells rang out again. The office was ending. Like every morning.

The nocturnal prayer expresses the monk's solitude. Courageous, humble, simple, he is alone facing life, facing death, facing eternity.

Monday, January 6, 2020
March of the kings

At 4:30 in the morning, I was awakened by the sound of bells. Ten minutes later, the matins of Epiphany would begin. Then the *Te Deum* at six o'clock, and the pontifical lauds at 6:10.

Last night, it froze. The moss on the linden trees in the courtyard was covered in frost, and the white roofs glistened in the dark night.

At the back of the church, about ten lay brothers were kneeling on the floor in front of the Nativity scene. Dom Antoine was praying alone beside the sacristy door. Soon, they would join the fathers to sing aloud:

> *Te Deum laudamus: te Dominum confitemur. Te aeternum Patrem, omnis terra veneratur. Tibi omnes Angeli, tibi caeli et universae potestates: tibi Cherubim et Seraphim, incessabili voce proclamant: Sanctus, Sanctus, Sanctus Dominus Deus Sabaoth. Pleni sunt caeli et ter-*

> *ra maiestatis gloriae tuae.* ("To you God, we praise you! We acclaim you as the Lord! Everlasting Father, hymn of the universe. Before you, the archangels, the angels, and the hosts of heaven prostrate themselves. They give you thanks; they worship you and they sing: Holy, Holy, Holy, Lord God of the universe; heaven and earth are filled with your glory.")

In the church, there wasn't a single worshiper. The few guests present stayed warm in their cells while the villagers or friends hadn't dared to brave the fog enveloping the countryside. So, the monks celebrated this solemn office alone in the dead of the night.

The long procession emerged from the sacristy. Dom Jean was mitered and carried a crosier; he wore a gold-colored cope. During the pontifical Mass, he would wear white leather caligae and gloves of the same color.

Incense wafted up in the choir. It couldn't be said that the monks wanted to impress the people, because the good folks were happily sleeping under their blankets. This night, the sons of Saint Benedict displayed the luxury of the liturgy for God alone. No one would know. And in this freezing temperature, the monks would also be just as comfortable in their beds.

On the high altar, adorned with silver threads, the tall candelabras were lit. The monks had placed lovely Christmas roses there, white and yellow. Dom Pateau was chanting an endless prayer; Dom Prior seemed to be watching for an invisible enemy in the distance; Dom Troupeau, the master of ceremonies, was searching desperately for a mysterious object in his pocket; and Dom Bernard was placing and removing the abbot's miter on his head.

Outside, the thermometer reading remained below freezing. In the abbey church, which had never known the comfort of winter heating since its construction in the medieval era, it was six degrees. The damp cold of the black river reigned supreme. It was enough to yawn a little, to wake up from sleep abandoned too early, to see a gentle, unsettling mist swirling around one's face.

The psalms flowed like waves. At 6:25, the monks began to chant the Canticle of the Three Youths. The abbey church was enveloped in lasting cold, and the weary stones heard these seemingly absurd words: "*Benedicite, rores et pruina, Domino: benedicite, gelu et frigus, Domino. Benedicite glacies et nives, Domino: benedicite, noctes et dies, Domino*": ("Bless the Lord, dews and hoarfrost; rime and wintry weather, bless the Lord. Bless the Lord, ice and snow; nights and days, bless the Lord.")

Later, with Psalm 148, the monks would say: "*Laudate Dominum de terra: / dracones et omnes abyssi. / Ignis, grando, nix, glacies, spiritus procellarum: / quae faciunt verbum ejus.*" ("Praise the LORD from the earth, / you sea monsters and all deeps, / fire and hail, snow and frost, / stormy wind fulfilling his command.") The voices of the monks in these long poems resembled the gentle sound of a small sandstorm. But we opened our eyes. And we were at Fontgombault. Outside, the night was still dark, deep, and silent, yet no less unfriendly.

Who is right? Who is a prophet? Who is mad? The men who sleep? The monks who sing and pontificate under the stars like lovers? Children love to draw endlessly for their parents. They play with all the colors. Monks are the same. They love to sing for their Father without ever stopping. They never tire. Night, day, days of drought, days of frost, days of celebration, days of sorrow, they sing.

In the stalls, I saw Dom François. He resembled a Carthusian. With his thick glasses, bushy eyebrows, and the weight of years bearing down on his shoulders, he had happily become an old monk.

Now 6:50: Lauds were coming to an end. Dom Pateau intoned the *Kyrie*, then the *Pater Noster*. Near the sanctuary entrance, a brother continued to send billows of incense heavenward. But large flames suddenly erupted from the censer, and the monk hurriedly retreated to the sacristy.

A few moments later, all the monks sitting at the throne withdrew along with the group at the lectern formed by the four cantors. The bells were ringing loudly, while a thick fog reached the doors of the abbey church.

In the village, the children would soon be waking up. Christmas vacation was over, and it was the first day back at school. At ten o'clock, they would be at school while the solemn Epiphany Mass began at the monastery. Inside the abbey church, the temperature had not risen much. The beautiful light of this winter day radiated through the blues and reds of the stained glass, reflecting as balls of fire on the choir walls.

Ten faithful participants awaited the Mass. Quite a crowd. The angelic voice of Brother Louis, the warm voice of Dom Pierre-Antoine, Dom Pateau's subdued voice — each was unique. The richness of the liturgical vestments inevitably evoked those of the Magi. The Epiphany Mass is unique and full of delicacy. The procession following the office of terce in the cloister is done in the opposite direction of the usual walk. Symbolically, the liturgy signifies that the monks follow the king *per aliam viam* ("by another way"): "And being warned in a dream not to return to Herod, they departed to their own country by another way" (Mt 2:12).

That morning, in the cloister's corridors, the monks formed a long, massive procession. They followed the kings, preceded by incense spirals. A young novice with a boyish face brought up the rear. However, he had taken the wrong position. Normally, it's Father Abbot who closes the procession, followed by the guests.

Similarly, at the end of the Gospel, the monks exceptionally genuflect to remind us that the kings prostrated themselves before the infant Jesus. Then, in a tone reminiscent of the *Exsultet* on Easter night, the first cantor proclaims the dates of the movable feasts for the upcoming year. It's an emotionally charged time of announcements.

After the universal prayer, Father Abbot blesses the galettes that will be consumed during the day's lunch. On this January 6, two monks brought the sweet treats in a basket protected by cotton. Dom Pateau sprinkled them with holy water using his aspergillum.

During his homily, he discussed the importance of stars in the history of Christianity. He told the faithful that "on every human life, a star shines." He even spoke of the path that the stars trace for us to the manger, the place of liberation from hectic lives.

In the refectory, amid the cold marble, after a hearty lunch, we enjoyed the galettes. In the morning, for breakfast, monks and guests had already tasted the delightful house-made brioches. But those who bit into the figurine shaped like the Virgin Mary did not leap with joy. At Fontgombault, no crowns are distributed; Benedictine life remains in control of its small, or large, emotions.

Saturday, May 30, 2020
The abbot's low Mass

At 6:55 in the morning, Dom Jean, hooded, arrived with quiet steps. There was a slight murmur in the abbey church, like an imperceptible noise.

Father Abbot, surrounded by two acolytes, one resembling an innocent child and the other a dreamy college student, paid it no mind. He was focused.

In the Chapel of the Holy Sacrament, his morning Mass began. Right next to it, in another chapel, Dom Prior was doing the same. At the high altar was the cellarer, grave and serious, as well. Everywhere, on the humble church altars, the monks were celebrating Mass. The Chapel of the Holy Sacrament is at the end of the abbey church. Its altar faces the East, the place of Christ's resurrection. On both sides are the tombstones of Father Abbot Édouard Roux and Father Abbot Jean Roy.

As every morning, the whispered words composed a comforting little tune. When the monks' breath left room for silence, the birds could be heard. A golden light that pierced through the stained glass played on the floors; curiously, it stopped right at the feet of an old monk attending Father Abbot's Mass.

Nothing of Dom Jean's spoken words could be heard. By observing his gestures, though, I could tell where he was in the service. The two acolytes exchanged an amused look. It was impossible to discern the insignificant mistake they had surely just made.

Around 7:10, Dom Pateau began the recitation of the Canon of the Mass. Ten minutes later, the monk and the two brothers approached and knelt on the white stone step of the altar to receive Communion.

As they prepared to receive the Host, they repeated the centurion's words from the Gospel of Matthew: "*Domine, non sum dignus ut intres sub tectum meum, sed tantum dic verbo et sanabitur anima mea.*" ("Lord, I am not worthy to have you come under my roof; but only say the word, and my servant will be healed" [Mt 8:8]). They struck their chests so forcefully that I could hear a dull thud. Before Dom Jean placed the Host on their tongues, they kissed his ring. Then, as Father Abbot delicately presented the Host, they held a silver plate beneath their chins.

After the Eucharist, everything happened very quickly. The final prayers at the altar, the *Ite missa est*, the blessing, the last

Gospel. My vision blurred slightly.

At 7:25, when Dom Jean returned to the main sacristy, a delightful scent of damp hay had filled the abbey church. The countryside and the church, the trees and the stones, the breath of the wind, the breath of the monks, all became one.

I vaguely thought of the Gospel of Mark: "So they are no longer two but one flesh. What therefore God has joined together, let no man put asunder" (10:8–9).

Saturday, May 30, and Sunday, May 31, 2020
If the Spirit blows

The sky was vivid blue, the sun beamed its rays, and the abbey church bent under an unusually soft light. On this Saturday, the first vespers of Pentecost marked the beginning of the celebrations that would commemorate the descent of the Holy Spirit upon the apostles.

Peace, calm, and serenity seized the heart. Perhaps this is what allows the Holy Spirit to descend upon this earth: the wings of white doves have all the graces, but they are fragile. They need to be awaited.

Evening melodies often have the charm of gentle breezes. This Saturday evening, however, we were quickly awakened by the solemn, firm, and supplicant tones of the *Veni, Creator*.

In Rome, at the Pantheon, for Pentecost, thousands of rose petals are released through the oculus of the great dome. They flutter and gently fall onto the marbles of the beautiful edifice. Here, on the banks of the Creuse, swirls of incense rise in large cumulus clouds to the sound of Gregorian chant. The monks are singing children who welcome the Spirit like joyful cherubs.

The next day, matins would begin at 4:40 in the morning. And lauds would follow an hour and a half later. The night office is the time of slowness. It's no longer the time of sleep, but the hour of monks keeping watch. Between matins and lauds, a blue light gradually emerged. The *Te Deum* chant changed the course of time. The organ thundered, and the voices proclaimed with strength:

> *Te per orbem terrarum sancta confitetur Ecclesia, Patrem immensae maiestatis; venerandum tuum verum et unicum Filium; Sanctum quoque Paraclitum Spiritum. Tu rex gloriae, Christe. Tu Patris sempiternus es Filius. Tu, ad liberandum suscepturus hominem, non horruisti Virginis uterum.* ("The Holy Church acknowledges your greatness, throughout the extent of the universe, O Father of infinite majesty! It also loves your true and only Son; and the comfort of the Holy Spirit. O Christ! You are the King of glory. You are the everlasting Son of the Father. When you took it upon yourself to deliver man, you did not disdain the Virgin's womb.")

Sometimes, one gets the impression that the monks spend their lives singing this solemn hymn of thanksgiving composed at the end of the fourth century. France, freshly emerged from lockdown, was still asleep, numbed by a nasty illness, and the monks sang ceaselessly from age-old texts.

How can one reach such a peaceful state? These prayer times are the opposite of a theatrical performance. Prayer is a diamond in the rough in the delicate sentiments of the monks.

The chapter from the office of lauds said: "The days of Pentecost being fulfilled, the disciples were all gathered in one place. And suddenly there came a sound from heaven, as of a rushing mighty wind, and it filled the whole house where they were sitting" (see Acts 2:1–2). At Fontgombault, there was no violent wind during those hours. Was it a refreshing breeze? No, rather the beginning of the wind.

During lauds, the long succession of psalms seemed never-ending. The monks asked the Spirit to enlighten their souls. But the Spirit is not bound by time. That is why, on that morning, time seemed to fade away in the abbey. It wasn't the first time. The monks are accustomed to losing track of time. Day is night, summer is winter. Only the search for God matters. The liturgical calendar is their compass. It is rich and precise because one must not stray.

Voices, hands joined, eyes lowered, incense, love, silence, Father Abbot: Pentecost resembled all the great feasts celebrated at Fontgombault. Nothing passed. Everything was ordinary. The extraordinary came from elsewhere. It had a face: that of purity.

For the Conventual Mass, at the throne Father Abbot was surrounded by an assisting priest, a deacon, and a subdeacon — or by a proud childlike Artaban, a dreamy poet and a gentle romantic.

On May 31, 2020, if the Holy Spirit had the sweet fragrance of a dove, no one could have smelled its innocent scent, except for the monks, as they did not wear masks.

Between the office of terce and the Mass, during the procession in the cloister, a monk usually reads a spiritual meditation. On this pandemic Sunday, after the long lockdown, they read out the health guidelines instead. Sacred hand sanitizer was made available everywhere in the abbey.

How can one edify the faithful with solemn faces? In a vigorous sermon, Father Abbot asked: "Why this illness? Who is responsible?" He pointed to the reckless pursuit of a man-god with Promethean desires. He added, "God always forgives, man sometimes, nature never." Dom Jean chose to condemn without ambiguity the man enslaved to the all-powerful market of liquid societies. His words had the merit of awakening the masked assembly.

During lunch in the refectory, they enjoyed the delicious

dishes of Brother Hervé-Marie, and they drank, in moderation, sparkling rosé and champagne. The monk knows how to live. He has a sense of time. Ordinary time, festive time. He has a sense of measure. Like the Holy Spirit.

For the last vespers, Dom Jean wore the same red silk cope, adorned with gold, that came from the Dutch abbey of Oosterhout. It was the same liturgy, the same pomp, the same light as on Saturday. There was one difference, however. Twenty-four hours had passed: one day less before the monk found the One he had been searching for all his life.

To conclude these festive days and close vespers, the organ exulted and played the hymn *Veni, Creator* by Nicolas de Grigny, with the theme on the pedals, in long notes, on the reeds …

Thursday, June 11, 2020
Corpus Christi again

The time of Corpus Christi had come again. Everything was different, everything was the same. Closing my eyes, I felt like it was June 20, 2019.

Dried flowers; wildflowers, yellow, red, purple, blue, white; rose petals; bouquets of roses, lilies; delicate fragrances; geometric figures; busy monks, hurried monks, monks running late, monks with smiles on their lips, monks in overalls; skilled novice workers, shy novices, red faces; hammer blows, twists of screws, saws, bolts, drills; stars; multicolored rose window; carpet of leaves, carpet of paradise; thickets of cut branches; organist at work; precise gestures, repeated gestures, gestures of the earth, gestures of heaven; threatening clouds, black clouds, June breeze, wind in the cypresses, wind in the pines; cooing of doves; tinkling of bells, peal of bells; procession, procession cross, procession faces; white albs, cowls, miters, croziers, candelabras, smoke; a cloud of light, a cloud of incense, incense spirals; roaring organ, meditative organ; genuflections, hands joined, heads bowed; Gregorian voices, angelic voices; *Kyrie, Gloria, Credo, Sanctus, Pater Noster, Agnus Dei*; ciborium, paten, chalice, spice scent; Father Abbot, assisting priest, deacon, subdeacon, cantors, Dom Forgeot, young monks, old monks; silent music; chasubles, cope; seven-branched candlesticks, candles, candlelight, wax fragrance; monstrance; ombrellino; blessing of the Blessed Sacrament; and *Tantum Ergo*. "Joy, joy, joy, tears of joy,"* peace, happiness.

But who are these monks who bring down a few drops of heaven to our earth?

* Blaise Pascal, *Pensées*, éd. Brunschvicg, Paris, Garnier, 1960.

III
Sing, Always Sing to God

Gregorian chant is an odyssey. We leave the sad world of men, we brave storms with heroism, we sail in calm seas, we lose ourselves in the most beautiful sunsets, and when the horizon of the solid earth appears, we already regret returning. For we want to continue seeking God.

I could confess that my ears are too accustomed to Fontgombault's Gregorian chant. Some speak of it as robust music, but I have never felt that way. Gregorian chant is gentle like a child, fragile like a flower, supple like a reed. Its depth gives it an unmatched strength. What a surprise to hear Gregorian chant's austerity: It is so strange to confuse spiritual simplicity, born of sought-after asceticism, with severity, rigor, and harshness. Gregorian chant is a chant of love, a poetic declaration.

The Berrichonne countryside — its fields, its cows, and its little paths — possess all the charms. But why, in this hidden place, do the monks sing God's compositions so perfectly?

By the banks of the Creuse, as the abbey becomes melancholic during the bleak winter days, the chant is a miracle that warms the chilled bodies. The strength of Gregorian chant serves as a heater.

On January 1, for vespers on the Solemnity of Mary, Holy Mother of God, the antiphon *O admirabile*, the hymn *Christe Redemptor ominum*, or the verse *Notum fecit* reach unparalleled beauty.

Do the monks truly realize it? They are like the inhabitants of the banks of the Seine who no longer saw the Cathedral of Notre-Dame de Paris because they were so accustomed to its grace. On the evening of the fire in 2019, they understood the great blessing of being neighbors with this marvelous monument.

Yet, one only needs to observe the people entering the abbey during the services. At the first chanted notes, their pace changes. They walk softly, disturbed, dazzled. They no longer know. With faces drawn toward the choir, everyone intimately senses that something greater is at play.

Gregorian chant is the realm of prayer. It can also be the realm of tears. These tears are not bitter. During Gregorian chant, in the stream of voices that exalt, adore, and implore, any person can surrender. They become like a child unafraid. Their mother watches over them.

In one verse, Rainer Maria Rilke wrote, "Only praise opens a space for lament." The soul of Gregorian chant lies here. It is a marvelous and selfless praise. It is priceless. The monks' voices open up painful spaces because Gregorian chant reveals man to himself. Through it, the veil is torn. It purifies. It gently pushes open the doors of mystery. Paul Verlaine marveled at "the inflection of beloved voices that have fallen silent."* Gregorian chant

* Paul Verlaine, "*Mon rêve familier*," in *Poèmes saturniens*, edited by Alexandre Gefen, (Paris: Larousse, 2004).

allows us to hear the inflection of the voices of those we will see in heaven. They are distant echoes. But heaven is already here.

The monk lives with Gregorian chant every day. He spends his life singing. It is a big mistake to consider this as nothing. The son of Saint Benedict scrupulously follows the *Rule* and remembers his words: "In the presence of angels, I will sing psalms to you." The brothers never tire; Gregorian chant is an unsuspected field of freedom. In the presence of angels, everything is possible.

At Fontgombault, the practice of Gregorian chant is rooted in the long Solesmes tradition. Trained by their motherhouse, the first Fontgombault monks naturally retained their old liturgical traditions. The Sarthe and the Creuse did not want to part ways.

The first Fontgombault superior, Dom Édouard Roux, was attached to the method known as Solesmes, taught by Dom André Mocquereau and Dom Joseph Gajard. Dom Roux wrote to the latter on September 5, 1939: "It is indeed true that I have always loved, approved, and encouraged, in all simplicity and candor because I need only see true prayer in it, your way of interpreting Gregorian chant. There is also a Solesmes tradition that we must not let perish."

These lines became the golden thread of Gregorian practice at Fontgombault. For nearly seventy-five years, the four abbots have been committed to preserving this tradition, and the monks have followed this guiding principle.

The fathers sing Gregorian chant to better pray. Vatican II's Constitution on the Sacred Liturgy states, "The Church acknowledges Gregorian chant as especially suited to the Roman liturgy: therefore, other things being equal, it should be given pride of place in liturgical services" (*Sacrosanctum Concilium*, 116).

In the Berrichonne abbey, the young prior is also the choirmaster. To speak of Gregorian chant, Dom Jean-Baptiste likes to quote Pope Benedict XVI, who wrote in a letter to the chancellor of the Pontifical Institute of Sacred Music, "To understand the monks' chant, one must remember that the celebration of the liturgy, which is their primary activity, is an action of God through the Church" (May 13, 2011).

Listening to the monks, one wonders how they can achieve such vocal perfection. Certainly, the abbey's acoustics are exceptional. But all arts demand painful discipline. Hours of work, moments of discouragement, and breakthroughs follow one another. Gregorian chant is no exception to this rule. Daily experience is the best training. It is essential to work: Gregorian chant is not something that can be improvised.

At Fontgombault, instruction is given in weekly chant classes. On Saturday evenings, the choir fathers attend a class lasting twenty-five minutes. For the past three years, the lay brothers have joined once a month. These lessons cover a variety of topics. The choirmaster may have them rehearse a few pieces. He addresses the most pressing issues: difficult solfeggio, delicate style, complex pieces. Study, reading, and applying musical commentary, or listening to recordings, especially those from Solesmes, are excellent ways to improve the choir.

The schola cantorum, composed of the abbey's chanters, has an additional weekly chant class of about thirty minutes. It is more technical due to the level and limited number of chanters. There are eight brothers in the schola, six who sing at Mass, and two others who fill in when one is occupied with another duty. The schola is the driving force responsible for training the choir.

Novices receive additional training, especially substantial for choir novices. They attend courses at the *Schola Saint-Grégoire*, an international academy of sacred music associated with the Solesmes method. Finally, once a year, the monks participate in vocal technique and Gregorian chant sessions.

Father Abbot is categorical: "This work has only one purpose: prayer." To pray well, one must sing well, and to sing well, one must work. The first Fontgombault choirmaster, Dom Jacques Lonsagne, wrote in 1956 in the *Revue grégorienne*:

> Watch the singer without theory. At every moment, he is in trouble. He knows the intervals by heart because he is ignorant of solfeggio. But the multiple nuances of rhythm surprise him at every moment. His art is fragile because it is devoid of a main idea, forced at every moment to rethink everything. The chanted prayer of the Church cannot be savored without preparation. ... The Church does not reject any form of prayer. But Gregorian chant is its language, that of the children of the house. ... In a family, there are known habits, words, looks, intonations, gestures that a guest for a day cannot understand. It is in such an atmosphere that the influence of technical means on this more perfect prayer, which we call, without too much strictness of the term, contemplation, becomes real and understandable.

• • •

The roots of Gregorian chant are lost in the early history of the Church. From its earliest origins, the prayer of Christ's disciples was accompanied by chant. The early Christians, coming from Judaism, retained the synagogue customs, both for the texts, especially the psalms, and for the melodies. The words of Saint Paul the Apostle are eloquent: "Let the word of Christ dwell in you richly, as you teach and admonish one another in all wisdom, and as you sing psalms and hymns and spiritual songs with thankfulness in your hearts to God" (Col 3:16). Also, "[Address] one another in psalms and hymns and spiritual songs, singing and making melody to the Lord with all your heart" (Eph 5:19).

Even a pagan writer like Pliny the Younger wrote: "[The arrested Christians] stated that their entire fault or mistake was limited to meeting regularly on a fixed day [Sunday] before dawn, and singing among themselves a hymn to Christ as to a god."* Furthermore, the first Christian liturgy in Jerusalem was certainly in Aramaic.

Originally, Christian worship spread at the same time as the preaching of the Gospel, all around the Mediterranean basin. Eastern regions that did not speak Greek celebrated in their own language and with their own rites. The diversity of surviving Eastern rites today attests to this richness.

In the Greco-Latin world, Greek initially became the liturgical language. The Western Church celebrated in Greek until the third century. The transition to Latin was not completed until the fourth century. A truly Christian liturgical chant was developed in the West, influenced by Jewish, Greek, and Latin traditions.

Dom Gajard, Solesmes Abbey's choirmaster from 1914 to 1970, distinguishes two stages in the development of Christian chant before the third century. He speaks of the diction phase, when the chant was merely an accentuation of the word to emphasize it, and then of the first melody rudiments that punctuate the text with accents and cadences. This is the origin of the monastic psalm tones, dating from the fifth, sixth, and seventh centuries, as well as the verses for lauds and vespers from the third and fourth centuries.

Very quickly, a sacred chant repertoire was formed in Latin, with different melodies and texts depending on the region: "Old Roman" chant; "Beneventan" chant in Southern Italy; "Milanese," or "Ambrosian," chant, named after Saint Ambrose, bishop of Milan in the fourth century; "Hispanic," or "Mozarabic," chant; "Gallican" chant. Except for Milanese chant, which has survived

* Pliny the Younger, Letter to Trajan, book 10, letter 96.

to this day with its specific rite, all other repertoires eventually disappeared. These were the ancestors of Gregorian chant.

The Milan Edict, signed by Emperor Constantine in 313, ended the Christian persecutions and ushered in a new era. The life of the Church could now flourish openly. It was the era of constructing the first basilicas, and the liturgy began to thrive. Between the fifth century and the mid-seventh century, liturgical chant followed the same development. During this time, *scholae cantorum*, made up of clerics capable of composing and performing increasingly elaborate pieces, emerged in various places. Liturgical chant experienced a great period of composition. The processional chants of the Mass, the introit, offertory, and Communion, as well as the alleluia, appeared at the end of the fourth century. The tract, and gradual, older pieces, probably took their definitive form between the fifth and seventh centuries. Some dialogues, like that of the preface, are inherited from the synagogue. The listener is struck by the magnificent continuity of these pieces.

Inheriting the intelligence of this movement, St. Gregory the Great (d. 604) left his name to the chant of the Latin Church. While he did not literally compose Gregorian music, he certainly contributed his own genius to the organization of the liturgy and liturgical chant of the Roman Church. The authenticity of the term "Gregorian chant" should be understood in the sense of these verses inscribed in a chant book from the early ninth century: "Taking up the books of his predecessors, he renewed and increased the pieces of chant contained in the offices throughout the year."

The golden age of Gregorian chant occurred between the eighth and tenth centuries. During the time of Pepin the Short, the papacy drew closer to the Frankish kingdom. The primary goal was political: The Papal States were threatened by the Lombards, so the pope sought the support of the Franks. On the other side, Pepin found moral support for his authority in the papacy. Their political rapprochement had practical spiritual consequences; the Carolingian leader ordered the adoption of the Roman liturgy in the Frankish kingdom. This alliance was decisive for chanting. Bishops from Gaul, probably Saint Chrodegang of Metz and Remedius of Rouen, who was Pepin's half-brother, and later Charlemagne himself, brought chanters from Rome to train the Frankish *scholae*.

The chant transmission was entirely oral. Manuscripts contained only the text; music was not yet notated. Historians believe that musicians from the Carolingian Empire must have composed new melodies for the Roman liturgy texts. To do this, they likely enriched the Old Roman chant with the chant from transalpine regions, especially that of northern Frankish Gaul, centered on the thriving centers of Aix-la-Chapelle, Rouen, Reims, and Metz. A hybrid repertoire spread throughout the empire and beyond, supplanting the old traditions. The widespread dissemination of this repertoire made it necessary to fix the melody. Gregorian chant and all of Western music then underwent a historical turning point.

The earliest known record of a written Mass chant is a manuscript from around the year 800. It contains only the text. The documents used by chanters in ceremonies were small scrolls held in hand. In Lyon, this practice took place until the eighteenth century. The oldest parchment showing neumatic notation — neumes are the signs representing the notes, without indicating the intervals of the melody — is the so-called Cantatorium of Saint Gall (cod. sang. 359), dating from the ninth or early tenth century. Originally, the term "antiphonary" referred to all chant books, even if they contained only text. By the late eighth century, the *Antiphonale missae* for the Mass, or *Antiphonale*, and the *Antiphonale officii*, or *Responsoriale*, for the entire office were distinguished. Then, extracts appeared: the *Gradale*, or *Cantatorium*, for soloists who sang from the ambo steps. By the late Middle Ages, the current names prevailed: the Gradual, which corresponds to the *Antiphonale missae*, the Antiphonal for the daytime office, and the *Responsoriale* for the nighttime office.

Manuscripts with diastematic notation, meaning they included intervals, appeared toward the end of the eleventh century thanks to Guido of Arezzo (d. 1033). This Benedictine monk can be considered the author of the staff and the *C* clef. He replaced the letters used until then — still in use in Anglo-Saxon countries — with the first syllables of each hemistich of the first stanza of the hymn of St. John the Baptist: "*Ut queant laxis Resonare fibris Mira gestorum Famuli tuorum, Solve polluti Labii reatum, Sancte Ioanne*": ("So that your servants may, with loosened voices, resound the wonders of your deeds, clean the guilt from our stained lips, O Saint John").

From the eleventh to the fifteenth century, musical production developed rapidly. Two new genres emerged: syllabication and polyphony. Syllabication involved putting words under the long vocalizations of Gregorian chant, also called melismas, by matching one syllable per note. Sequences — developments based on the themes of the *alleluia* vocalizations — and tropes — lyrics to the notes of the ordinary pieces like the *Kyrie* — were born during this time before becoming independent proses. New books were written to correspond to these genres: sequentiaries, troparies, and prosaries, which were different from one church to another and typical of the Frankish liturgy. Rome remained reluctant to these new pieces, and the Tridentine reform practically eliminated this entire repertoire, preserving only five sequences, of about five thousand compositions, for the Masses of the year: *Victimae paschali* at Easter, *Veni Sancte Spiritus* at Pentecost, *Lauda Sion* at Corpus Christi, *Dies Irae* for the deceased, and *Stabat Mater* for the feast of Our Lady of Sorrows.

The appearance of sacred polyphony began first with organum, the addition of a second voice at the fourth or lower fifth. Then, counterpoint developed, a more complex second voice where the melody crossed *punctum contra punctum*.

However, if polyphony produced true masterpieces, it gradually moved further away from its model and hastened its decline. The Gregorian melody was gradually distorted, with the measured rhythm of polyphony taking the place of the free rhythm of Gregorian chant. Nevertheless, only the performance was altered; the manuscript tradition remained intact until the reform of the chant books after the Council of Trent.

In 1577, Pope Gregory XIII (r. 1572–85) appointed a team of Roman musicians, led by the great composer Giovanni Pierluigi da Palestrina (1525–94), to prepare a new chant-book edition. This recomposition work was not published, thanks to the intervention of Philip II of Spain: "Do not allow such an insult to occur in the very homeland and under the pontificate of another Gregory!"

Taken up by another composer, Giovanni Guidetti, the work eventually resulted in the first edition of a modernized chant in 1588, completely overhauled: shortened vocalizations, use of bar lines, proportional notation (whole notes, half notes, and quarter notes), an accumulation of notes on accents at the expense of finals.

The "Medicean" Gradual edition adopted the same principles but took them to an extreme. Printed by Cardinal Ferdinand de Medici in 1614 and tolerated by Pope Paul V, this whimsical Gradual achieved great success. It became the archetype for all musical plainchant books. No one dared to speak of Gregorian chant in the centuries that followed. So much so that, at the beginning of the nineteenth century, all available editions were poor. It was then that Dom Prosper Guéranger had the insight that the restoration of the Roman liturgy in France should be accompanied by a renewal of Gregorian chant.

In the seventeenth and eighteenth centuries, the dioceses of France had created their own liturgy. Dom Guéranger was convinced that the Church's chant could only be beautiful, far removed from anything that could be heard in his time in plainchant. He also understood that it was necessary to return to the oldest manuscripts to rediscover the original purity of sacred chant. He already explained this principle in 1840, in his famous *Institutions liturgiques*: "It is obvious that sometimes we have the right to believe that we possess the Gregorian phrase in its purity in a particular piece when the copies from several distant churches agree on the same lesson."* It was necessary, therefore, to be able to decipher the manuscripts, something that no one had succeeded in doing until then.

The Solesmes monks, under his impetus, accomplished a veritable Benedictine work. The task was to copy, then photograph, all available manuscripts throughout Europe to be able to compare them and restore the melodies. Dom Paul Jausions was the first to take on the task, later joined by Dom Joseph Pothier.

Solesmes' goal was, above all, to be able to sing the office. Therefore, Dom Pothier edited a *Liber gradualis* in 1883. In order to defend Dom Pothier's book, Dom Mocquereau (1849–1930), the theoretician of the Solesmes method, launched the *La Paléographie musicale* collection, which presented facsimiles of the main manuscripts, gathered and demonstrated the conformity of Solesmes' edition with tradition.

On November 22, 1903, Pope St. Pius X issued the motu proprio *Tra Le Sollecitudini* on sacred music. This text marks a significant reversal in approach. For the new pope, Gregorian chant was to regain its primary place in the liturgy. In 1904, a commission was formed under the presidency of Dom Pothier, then abbot of Saint-Wandrille, with the aim of restoring Grego-

* Dom Prosper Guéranger, *Institutions liturgiques*, 3 vol., (Paris: Débécourt, 1840–1851).

rian chant and publishing a Vatican edition. Dom Mocquereau and the workshop of musical paleography at Solesmes, consisting of twelve full-time monks, were entrusted with the task. However, differences between Dom Pothier and Dom Mocquereau regarding the melody restoration — with Dom Pothier allowing alterations — led to Solesmes being excluded from the project from 1905 to 1913. Gregorian battles could sometimes be quite disappointing. The commission led by Dom Pothier published the *Roman Gradual* (1908), the *Officium Defunctis* (1909), and the *Roman Antiphonary* (1912).

Starting in 1913, Solesmes was once again entrusted with the work, which resulted in the publication of the *Cantus Passionis* (1916), the *Officium Majoris Hebdomadae et Octavae Paschae* (1922), the *Officium et Missae in Nativitate Domini* (1926), and the *Antiphonale Monasticum* (1934).

From the pontificate of St. Pius X to the Second Vatican Council, the promotion of Gregorian chant bore visible fruit in the Catholic Church. *Scholae* multiplied, and meetings on sacred music were frequent. The council expressed a clear preference for the use of the Latin language and Gregorian chant, while allowing for the use of vernacular languages.

However, in the late 1960s, there was a decline in the practice of Gregorian chant, despite the desires expressed by Pope Paul VI, especially in the apostolic letter *Sacrificium Laudis* of August 15, 1966, addressed to the superiors of religious orders bound to the choir office:

> We must not underestimate what the ancients created who, over many centuries, brought you glory. This organization of the choral office was one of the main causes of the strength and successful development of your communities. It is surprising, therefore, that a sudden surge of fever leads some to now want to neglect it.

During this period of decline, the papal magisterium continued to periodically present Gregorian chant as a reference and to recommend its wider use. However, it remained marginalized in practice.

Today, the desire for a return to the sources, though not official in the field of chant, is widely validated by the enthusiasm for manuscripts. In fact, it is essential to return to the earliest "partitions" if one wants to rediscover the purity of Gregorian chant.

While it may seem like a debate for experts, Gregorian chant holds significant importance in the life of abbeys, and it is at the heart of the daily routine for monks. Controversies regarding its origins, the place of beauty in liturgy, and the importance of Latin fuel endless discussions inside the monastic communities.

• • •

During a long and insightful conversation, Fontgombault's choirmaster shared:

> Historical research is valuable to understand the spirit in which the liturgy, which is not fabricated but received from the Church, should be lived. As Pius XI wrote, history is the "teacher of life." The liturgy and the sacred chant intrinsically linked to it are living realities. They evolve over time in an organic and homogeneous development. In other words, my interest is not in singing Gregorian chant as it was sung in the ninth century, but in having the Fontgombault choir sing the Gregorian chant that we have in our liturgical books given by the Church. This doesn't mean we should stop researching, but we cannot allow just anything. Gregorian chant in the twenty-first century has inevitably enriched itself

with centuries of musical culture compared to the Gregorian chant of the ninth century. There is a genuine tradition here. Gregorian chant evolved throughout its history. Singing Gregorian chant today means not so much trying to rediscover how the ancients sang but rather participating in this tradition. If we want to do a historical reconstruction, then let's sing like they did in the ninth century. But no one knows exactly how they sang. … The enrichment of Gregorian chant should be understood more from the side of the singers than the chant itself. The work of restoring chant is essential, but it will not provide us with all the interpretation nuances that can only be acquired through listening. The manuscripts are filled with rhythmic signs that it is illusory to try to reproduce entirely. Listening, the musical knowledge of twenty-first-century cantors, has benefited by everything that polyphony, classical music, in short, all Western music born from Gregorian chant, has brought. Whether we like it or not, Gregorian chant today is necessarily different from the past. Furthermore, there is no consensus on how to sing it. However, we should not aim for a single interpretation. Unity does not mean uniformity, and differences in the interpretation of pieces are legitimate. In this regard, the Solesmes method has its place, just like others. Moreover, it needs to be further explored and better understood and practiced. It's not an unbearable straitjacket. It's too often the caricature of the method that is criticized. We must avoid a systematic approach that would lead to developing studies in semiotics or freezing a method, while ignoring legitimate discoveries. Our contemporary ears and musical sensibilities have evolved compared to those of our ancestors. Nevertheless, there must be no rupture.

> This is the entire issue of knowing how to inherit, to carry on the patrimony of sacred music, [above all] the spirit in which we must live it. To resolve this, we must realize that the liturgy and Gregorian chant are living realities that do not belong to us, because they are the expression of the very life of the Church.

In Fontgombault Abbey's library, Dom Pateau, a renowned expert in Gregorian music, added:

> Fr. Louis Bouyer wrote that "authentic tradition is nothing other than the transmission, throughout the existence of the people of God, of this same light and life tradition that has been deposited in the Bible itself." The same can be said of sacred chant. Singing Gregorian chant today only makes sense if one is part of this living current, this living tradition, this transmission of sacred chant from its origin to the present day. And one can be part of this current only within the liturgical framework. Gregorian chant has no meaning outside of its vital element, which is the liturgy. Monastic tradition is a great river that originates in God himself but enriches itself with everything that Christian centuries can bring.

The crucial point is not to seek out the purest form of Gregorian chant. The Fontgombault Benedictines reject archaeology. They study the past not to vainly attempt to resurrect it, but to live in the present. True tradition consists of aligning oneself with a current that comes from the depths of ages and remains alive. The fundamental issue lies elsewhere. It concerns the concept of beauty and its encounter with liturgy. For Father Abbot, "This issue is crucial":

> To address it, we would first need to define the terms. However, it is very difficult to define liturgy because it is a living reality. We do not define life; we can only attempt to describe it. The holy liturgy, preeminently in the Eucharist, makes present at every moment in history the paschal mystery of Christ, his death and resurrection, the sacrifice that redeems and enlivens us. The true subject of the liturgy, the sole high priest, is Christ himself. We are only his servants, his ministers, and at the same time Christ makes us his friends because he shares his life with us. Liturgy is the path we must take to reach God through Christ. The goal of our Christian life is union with God, and this union is obtained through prayer and conformity to the divine will. Therefore, liturgy is the path par excellence because it is the Church's prayer itself and the place where we are assured of encountering God and doing his will, by praising, thanking, and adoring him, by offering him worship "in spirit and in truth." It is, therefore, a path, but here on earth we approach the intelligible and the spiritual through the sensible. We need external, material signs and symbols to introduce us to spiritual realities.

The work of the paleography workshop at Solesmes was necessary to collect, preserve, and decipher the manuscripts. The Sarthe Abbey undertook a herculean and prophetic task. Since then, some manuscripts have disappeared, and researchers can only find copies of them in Solesmes.

An odd question burned in my mind. Can one be a monk if one does not love Gregorian chant? Can a man with a true monastic vocation, a supernatural calling, experience a musical discomfort with Gregorian chant? According to the choirmaster:

> He will develop a taste for it if he approaches it generously. The most famous example is undoubtedly that of Dom Mocquereau at Solesmes. His initial encounters with Gregorian chant were painful. Dom Mocquereau was a talented musician; he had excelled as a cellist and seemed destined for a brilliant career before choosing monastic life. Gregorian chant disappointed him at first. The compositional rules of this unique chant bewildered him. However, that did not deter his superiors from sending him to study chant alongside Dom Pothier, whom he assisted for nearly a decade before being appointed choirmaster in 1889. I would like to read you a passage from Justine Ward that recounts Dom Mocquereau's "conversion" to Gregorian chant: "In the quiet of his cell, Dom Mocquereau was preparing an offertory for a martyr's feast: '*Posuísti Dómine in cápite ejus corónam de lápide pretióso*' ('You have placed on his head, O Lord, a crown of precious stones'). He softly hummed the melody and stopped, amazed and fascinated: 'Eh! This is music, real music, beautiful music!' He took his cello, tuned it, and played the melody *legato*; that was the moment of his conversion. The offertory *Posuísti* was the blinding light that changed the direction of his entire life, as in the conversion of Saint Paul. After having been the 'enemy' of Gregorian chant, Dom Mocquereau became its most fervent apostle."* He began working on Gregorian chant out of obedience, and this obedience led to his complete "conversion."

Without showing any repulsion for Gregorian chant, a monk may have no sense of music. A father from Fontgombault, now

* Dom Pierre Combes, *Justine Ward and Solesmes* (Washington, D.C.: The Catholic Universityof America Press, 1992).

deceased, couldn't string together three notes. He was faithful to the divine office, diligent in chant classes, and meticulously noted all the choirmaster's instructions. He preferred nothing to the work of God, as Saint Benedict instructs. But he couldn't sing. Moreover, military marches seemed to him the most complex form of musical composition.

Dom Jean-Baptiste commented candidly on this situation:

> We must be aware that Gregorian chant has an austere aspect. It is not easy, but it leads to the love of God. However, the life of grace, which is intimacy with God, does not destroy our humanity but evangelizes it. This culture needs appropriate music, which not just any musical genre can provide. In particular, it requires music that does not separate the profane from the spiritual, natural life from supernatural life.

Gregorian chant addresses the supernatural depths of the soul. This chant is not written to please the senses. That is why it's not always easy to enter its world, to understand its coherence. But the more the monks sing, the more they develop a taste for it. The repertoire returns every year, unchanged, with ever-fresh vitality. Music pacifies the being, even the most sensitive passions.

Cardinal Joseph Ratzinger, a lover of music and a pianist, reflected greatly on the eminent place of music in Catholic liturgy. In a book with a charmingly old-fashioned title, *A New Song for the Lord*, he established a true theory of music in which Gregorian chant took on its full value:

> There is music of agitation that leads man to serve various collective objectives. There is sensual music that sharpens erotic appetite or drives it toward other sensual pleasures. There is music purely for distraction, which

> has nothing to say and simply breaks the silence that has become too heavy. There is rationalist music whose melody serves only rational constructions, speaking neither to the spirit nor the senses. Some catechetical songs without soul, many modern songs crafted by committees, would likely belong in this category. The appropriate music for the worship of the God-made Man, exalted on the cross, draws its life from another synthesis, broader and of greater scope, a synthesis of spirit, intuition, and melody speaking to the senses. It can be said that Western music, from Gregorian chant to Bruckner and beyond, through cathedral music and great polyphony, through Renaissance and Baroque music, arises from the inner richness of this synthesis, which has unfolded in a multitude of possibilities. It is here alone that we find this greatness because it could only develop on the anthropological soil that united the spiritual and the profane into a final human unity. It dissolves as this anthropology fades away. The greatness of this music is, for me, the most immediate and obvious assessment of the Christian vision of man and the salvific Christian faith that history can offer us.

Greek music aimed to order souls. Gregorian chant may, perhaps, achieve the ideal dreamed of by ancient philosophers because of the use of another language, Latin. Fortunately, the importance of Latin is no longer a matter of debate. Its detractors have constantly questioned the value of preserving a dead language for liturgy. But perhaps the question should be: Is Latin truly a dead language, given that it is still used by the Church? According to Fontgombault's choirmaster, it's important to remember:

> Latin is the official language of the Church. All import-

> ant and official acts of the Church are written in Latin. It's interesting to hear that, while its official texts are written in Latin, some claim that the [Second Vatican] Council banned its use. Because it doesn't belong to any country, this language is well-suited to the Church. Latin transcends borders. Through its universality, the language of the Romans signifies the unity of the Church. Latin takes us out of time, connecting the Church of yesterday to the Church of today and tomorrow, just as it takes us out of space, connecting the Church in France to the Church in Korea, Senegal, or America. This language allows Catholics to speak the same language, to pray, and address God with the same words.

Indeed, Latin has never ceased to be the liturgical language of the Church. Because it is no longer the language of a particular country, Latin is reserved for speaking to God. Of course, heaven doesn't require Latin. When I asked about this, Dom Jean Pateau replied:

> Latin is for us, to help us understand that the words spoken in this language are important. They go beyond the ordinary. With Latin, we depart from the profane world, from the everyday, to enter another world, another universe, that of the things of God and the Church. That's why the Second Vatican Council, in the constitution *Sacrosanctum Concilium*, decided that "the use of the Latin language, except where a particular law requires or permits the use of the vernacular, must be preserved in the Latin rites." The practical elimination of Latin on the pretext that everyone must understand the words is a mistake. Through Latin, even without grasping every word, the faithful understand that something great

> and mysterious is taking place. In the church, we speak "l'abbé," as a choir boy once said, it's no longer everyday language.

Latin is a musical language, par excellence. Ecclesiastical Latin, descended from popular Latin, is built on tonic accents, whereas classical Latin is metric. The Latin musicality is evident at all levels: syllable, word, phrase. It is a rhythmic and resonant language. Gregorian chant was born from this musicality. Thus it is technically impossible to sing French melodies with Gregorian melodies. Why are there so many conflicts surrounding Gregorian chant? The choirmaster's response was quite radical:

> To understand the divisions regarding Gregorian chant, one must go back to the root cause —that is, to the ultimate divider, the devil. The devil does not like Gregorian chant, just as he detests liturgy. He cannot stand rhythm — that is, the order, the arrangement of movement. If there is music in hell, it can only be cacophonous. Rhythm is what connects the different parts that make up a movement and gives them life. Moreover, Gregorian chant is saturated with truth, as Dom Gajard said. It is a true chant, both in terms of its composition and its message. The devil does not like order or truth. He abhors anything that can bring us closer to God. So, he favors anything that can harm Gregorian chant, anything that can disfigure it. Of course, we should not attribute to the demon what is often the result of human folly. But in matters that touch religion most deeply, it is certain that Satan will fan the flames of division and rebellion.

In a mezza voce, speaking of music, a monk from Fontgombault had wisely told me that circumstances often generate multiple approaches to the same reality. It is not easy to discern the truth contained in each approach. Gregorian chant is no exception. Conflict often arises because one approach is favored over others, one element over others. The synthesis should not be lost sight of.

For the choirmaster:

> Conflict arises from a form of superficiality. We do not delve deep into things. Achieving synthesis means going back to the root, to what holds everything together. It must be recognized that it is not easy for a complex reality like Gregorian chant. If we keep the Church's perspective and take the well-being of the Church's sung prayer as the sole criterion, many difficulties fade away. Conflicts have their roots in ideology. We face ideology when the will holds intelligence captive and hinders the apprehension of reality as it is. Ideology no longer seeks to account for reality but only to justify its system. "Systems are based on abstractions," Dom Guéranger said. True freedom unfolds, on the contrary, when intelligence provides a framework for the will through the pursuit of truth. That's why only truth truly sets us free. If we apply this to Gregorian chant, it means that it is not enough to say that one theory is necessarily right against another. In scientific matters, one must remain open to all hypotheses and remain attentive to the objectivity of reality. When an interpretation of a piece does not make us pray, we must question ourselves. Regarding the opposition between advocates of voice and melody, it seems to me to be artificial. If some reject the organ, others sing just as well a cappella as accompanied by the organ. It just needs to be kept in its place.

In his *Diary of a Country Priest*, Georges Bernanos wrote, "Only from prayer can tears come that are not cowardly."* Gregorian chant is the enemy of falsehood. As the child of antiquity and the perfect freedom of its music, it is a wonder; with it, the self rises, is nourished, and falls silent.

* Georges Bernanos, *Diary of a Country Priest* (Paris: Plon, 1936).

IV
The Four Seasons

UNDER THE AUGUST SUN

The linden trees in the large courtyard no longer exhaled the wonderful scent of June. The yellowed grass, the red carpets of dried flowers, the hard earth, the warm walls betrayed the great work of the endless scorching summer. The tender landscapes of the Berry region were not accustomed to this battle. Most of the guests could barely conceal their fatigue from the hot days. The sun was relentless, and the blue sky bathed the abbey church. Yet the monks had not changed their tunics. They wore the same black woolen habit without complaint as they did in winter.

In the riverbed of the Creuse, the water level was visibly dropping. The power plant was no longer operational; the flow was too weak. A swarm of white waterlilies embraced the calm water.

In the evening, under the trees, some men lingered on scattered benches. They hoped to find a bit of coolness. Retreatants spoke one-on-one with a monk. Solitary individuals smoked cigarettes while reading books, and chatterers recounted their days. The encounter with a monk, the beauty of the liturgies, walks in the surrounding countryside, and the increasing heat in the rooms were all reasons to exchange a few words. The previous night, hunters had organized a chase on the other side of the river. They were probably tracking wild boars. Around midnight, gunshots rang out, and the echoes of the jubilant hunting dogs were heard for a long time. Everyone shared their anecdotes. One dreamt of jumping out of bed to join the hunt, while another wondered if the monks had been awakened. Conversations flowed freely.

Night fell, and it was time to return. The white stone staircase leading to the guesthouse had seen many such evenings. It wouldn't take offense at guests who did not observe the silence customary after compline. The good porter monk, whose cell was at the top of the stairs, slept the sleep of the righteous. The inscription in Gothic letters adorning the wall at the top of the steps took on its full meaning: "Peace and joy to this house."

At Fontgombault, the guests' breakfast is scheduled for half past eight. After the office of prime, they go to the small refectory overlooking the grand courtyard. In this somewhat gloomy room, long tables, a few old sideboards, and a faded tapestry seemed sufficient to the monks for their morning meal. Near the Philippe Poitevin stone fireplace, the meal is simple and hearty. Milk and butter from the farm, homemade coffee, bread from the monastery bakery, and jams made each summer from the fruits of the orchard make up this quiet meal. On this morning of August 9, the brothers had left the windows wide open to let in the morning freshness. Some birds offered joyful melodies. The scene, however, is less poetic in winter; dampness and gray light make the place depressing.

On their side, before prime, the monks have their first meal of the day, standing in the refectory. They never have butter, except on Sundays and major feasts, nor do they have jam. They simply consume, along with coffee, compotes, porridge, or yogurt.

With breakfast finished, the guests sought to enjoy the last moments of the mild temperature. In front of the abbey church's porch, a child who cared little about all this was learning to walk. His parents were on guard against any falls as older boys played hide-and-seek behind the trees of the grand avenue. At the back of the church, well-behaved little girls were waiting to go to confession.

The days resembled one another. The monks are the custodians of a happy monotony. On this morning, the heatwave did not alter the age-old schedules: the Conventual Mass, morning obediences — that is, tasks entrusted by a superior — the office of sext.

After lunch, I watched the monks leave for a walk on the narrow roads nearby. Under the fir trees, a small group from the novitiate choir sat on the grass around the master. On his part, the father guestmaster was conversing with families. But the bells were already ringing. At 2:35 in the afternoon, the office of none began.

In the afternoon, for hours on end, the organist played. He was rehearsing the pieces for the August 15 services. The notes of Handel's Seventh Organ Concerto in B Major and Bach's Grand Prelude in D Major gave the abbey church the appearance of an abandoned palace.

Outside, under the trees, a friendly Scottish family was shelling beans from the garden, placing them in large baskets. Another group was peeling hundreds of apples from the orchard. A monk brought a cold mint drink to encourage them. Near a tree, a young man was looking at family photos with his monk brother. Nearby, a monk wearing a straw hat looked quite elegant. He was diligently cleaning the garage doors. In the enclosure, passing teenagers were helping a whimsical young monk wearing clogs; the recruits were planting a new lawn. Gradually, the abbey had embarked on the restoration of its beautiful French-style gardens.

In the late afternoon, the rain began to fall. The fine drops brought long-awaited moisture. Everyone returned happily without asking for more.

The next day, the wind picked up. It swirled through the trees. The windows of the bakery overlooking the guesthouse garden were open. We could smell the scent of the bread baking in the oven. A delicious pasta aroma wafted through the air.

On the grass, a daring priest was seated behind a small table. From a distance, like a well-behaved child, he seemed to be doing holiday homework. But the gentle storm played with his papers. He had to give up, greeted a brother carrying baskets of vegetables, and went back into the church.

During the Mass, the imposing door of the abbey church remained open. The breath of fresh air seemed to delicately accompany the monks' chant. The fine and steady rain fell straight down.

In the park, joyful sounds emanated, including that of turtledoves. The farming monk was happy. It was the end of the drought. In the cloister, the boxwoods had been expertly trimmed. After sext, the long procession of monks moved from the church to the refectory. Water streamed down the slate roof. The walls were soaked. It took very little for Fontgombault to don its autumnal attire.

THE POETRY OF AUTUMN

On this November evening, night fell quickly. The countryside was enveloped in thick fog, and the abbey church resembled a solitary lighthouse. The white stones and the stained-glass windows' light imbued the last bluish drops falling from the sky with poetry. Inside the nave, it was surprising: neither cold nor warm.

Before compline, I had heard an owl hooting in the nearby orchard and the pleasant sound of an elderly faithful's rosary beads as he knelt before the statue of Our Lady of a Good Death. A novice had just left the community. He had received the religious habit, but the experience had not been a happy one. I observed him. His face was pained and melancholic. The young man was staying in the guesthouse for a few days before leaving the abbey. During the services, he had given up his place in the choir but continued to diligently follow the monks' prayers from the nave. In the morning, for breakfast, he joined the guest refectory. The secular world was slowly returning.

The silence of the guesthouse had changed. It was less gentle, more oppressive. Sometimes, soft footsteps could be heard in the long corridor. Outside, the golden colors of the countryside couldn't break through the sepulchral aura of the trees drenched by a passing little storm. From the window of my office, I saw a monk cleaning the large wooden barrels in one of the abbey's cellars. The wind blew, and the brother battled against the gusts. He worked courageously. A few moments later, I found myself in the church where the organist was rehearsing a piece. In all seasons, music resounded under the vaults.

The next day, after lunch, when the dishes were done, I saw the monks go for a walk. The low season didn't change their habits. Cold rain soaked the countryside, but it didn't discourage the monks. In small groups, they walked up to the old train station. Their attires were thoroughly soaked, but they didn't mind, saying, "Our tunics retain water well." That day, the monks had no luck. Just as they crossed the abbey's gate, the sun broke through the sky. The light glistened on the trees, and the golden leaves radiated.

The three retreatants staying in the guesthouse left for some work in the gardens. They had to collect the fallen leaves after the last gusts of wind. The former novice stayed inside and spent several hours in prayer in a chapel.

Outside, night was falling. A pale light fell on the village. The night was approaching. As I walked up to the departmental road, I saw smoke rising from the chimneys. The farmhouses in the hamlets seemed lost in the fields. For the moment, there was no frost. The heifers, calves, and cows were reluctant to return to the barn, while, slowly, night covered Fontgombault.

For dinner, served in the refectory, hot potato and carrot soup steamed. The brothers, wearing their large white aprons, placed large tureens in the middle of the tables. We dug into our food. A slight humidity hung in the air.

In the church, a large white curtain had been hung near the door leading to the cemetery to prevent drafts during the first cold spells. I wasn't convinced of the stratagem's effectiveness.

Before compline, the former novice waited alone for a long time in front of the cloister entrance gate, which he could no longer cross. A tear rolled down his face, and he hurried to find his handkerchief.

The nave sank into semi-darkness. Only the heights of the choir were illuminated. The abbey church was enveloped in a great silence.

The next morning, Brother Louis-Marie spent several hours harvesting beets in the garden. In a light drizzle, protected by an old worn-out overcoat, he worked without complaint. I noticed his wonderful childlike gaze and couldn't help but think, confusedly and stubbornly, that it resembled the eyes of the saints in heaven. Meanwhile, an old monk had set about dusting the church benches. He had three white cloths: one for the prie-dieu, one for the seats, and the last one for the backrests. It was essential to establish a strict difference between the types of dust.

The soft sound of the fabrics on the wood couldn't disturb the priest confessing to a monk. Only faint, distant, and imperceptible words could be heard.

At noon, in the refectory, the brother wearing clogs read from the pulpit *Les chrétiens dans al-Andalus: De la soumission à l'anéantissement* ("Christians in al-Andalus: from submission to annihilation") by historian Rafael Sánchez Saus. The monk, with an angelic face, a childlike smile, seemed to have escaped from a Cluniac stall. His strange and beautiful voice, crystalline, fine, and deep at the same time, let the pages of the day's reading flow. In the evening, in the dim light of the refectory, during the reading of the *Rule*, all the monks bowed their heads. They resembled the soft and hieratic alabaster mourners on the tombs of the Dukes of Burgundy. In the reader's chair, a monk read the chapter dedicated to the cellarer.

Before compline, I saw a figure advancing in the night. I recognized the farmer who had taken care of the calves that were born a few days ago. He greeted me with a friendly gesture. The night would be cold, the temperature would drop to two degrees Celsius. On November 7, it had not yet frozen, but the deep cold was approaching. The last office of the day was about to begin. In the church, there were only two retreatants. Once again, the monks chanted the office for God and not for the crowds. After Dom Prior's blessing, who had to stand in for Father Abbot in his absence, the bells rang loudly in the cold night.

The next day, in pouring rain, a brother was busy collecting the last tomatoes from the garden. They wouldn't withstand the first frost. The kitchen awaited the baskets.

The day passed quickly. At dusk, three hunters arrived at the abbey's gate. They brought a deer killed two hours earlier. In the afternoon, in the distance, toward the woods, gunshots and the howling of a pack of dogs could be heard. They called the brother who was the butcher; the small group examined the beast with its silky red fur. In a wooden crate, a trickle of blood escaped from its delicate head.

The men discussed how to cook the animal. Suddenly, in the sky, a strange noise was heard, and a colony of cranes were observed flying on the horizon. They were heading toward warmer lands. A hunter exclaimed, "They said on the radio this morning that it would freeze in a week." But the brother who was the butcher was skeptical. He expected it to happen in a few hours. However, his interlocutor was certain, "Marie heard it on the news, too."

The bells put an end to the debate. They were ringing for vespers. The light was fading. Everyone went back to their place. In the distance, the village lights were coming on.

During the night, it froze. The monk had been right. At dawn, we could see the white grass in the fields sparkling under the large golden blanket of autumn trees.

A FREEZING COLD

The call to the monastic life is a vocation. Little did I know that being cold was part of that.

On January 3, 2020, a gentle wind and a bit of sun warmed the countryside. But inside the church was a different story. The innkeeper thought it necessary to tell me that the cold could cause frostbite but added: "Winter is invigorating. It awakens the body." I was left speechless.

At the back of the church, the monks had set up a surprisingly imposing and simple Nativity scene. The organ resounded with Christmas pieces, and Georges Bizet's *March of the Kings* thundered through the vaults.

Outside, where it was more comfortable compared to the church, scouts from Paris were getting ready to leave the monastery. On their uniforms, the young boys wore navy blue woolen capes, as if they had just come out of a boarding school from the

1950s. In the guesthouse library, Dom Jean was giving a lecture to young married men. They attentively listened to the master's teaching, each having taken care to cover themselves with a thick coat. Father Abbot was focused, his audience diligently taking notes with numb hands.

During a brief stay at the monastery, a pulmonologist from a large Parisian hospital told me straight out: "The monks are either heroes or superhumans. Medically speaking, I can't explain how they endure the winter. The warmth of faith must cover everything. Often, I leave with a sore throat."

At Fontgombault, Saturday is a cleaning day. Monks would regularly appear at the windows. One would shake his dust cloth, another would beat a large rug against the wall. In the cloister, a young novice removed cobwebs from the vaults with a brush. Then he used a very noisy vacuum cleaner to clean the floors. He worked tirelessly. It must have warmed him up.

During vespers, the damp cold literally oozed from the walls. The black stained-glass windows seemed to protect the monks from the gusts battering the countryside. The mist from the breath of the retreatants almost erased their faces. The choir organ accompanied the chant; it was the most reassuring presence in a usually gentle service.

Near the refectory, almost as cold as the cloister, potato and carrot soups were steaming in heavy tureens that the monks quickly brought in. One shouldn't dream too much. The plates cooled quickly, and the old monks kept pressing large white handkerchiefs to their noses.

During the reading of Saint Benedict's Rule, the monks always looked like statues. In autumn, they looked like wax statues; in winter, they seemed more like ice sculptures.

The monks appeared tired. With pale complexions, slower movements, and circles under their eyes they were different. How could the older ones accept such conditions? In the abbey church, after dinner, Dom Antoine continued his evening work. At the age of eighty-seven, he faithfully carried it out. I saw him with his duster, picking up pieces of melted candles from the floor. The temperature inside the building didn't exceed six degrees.

To endure this cold, one must become a little robot, an automaton that moves forward without asking questions. At Sunday Mass, the children had pulled their turtleneck sweaters up to their noses. They looked like gangsters.

The battle against the cold is a fight against death. It must prevent the body from becoming as rigid as frozen wood. With frozen feet, the monk fights against the impressive slowing of his blood circulation.

Fortunately, the organ played the Nativity pieces with enthusiasm. *March of the Kings* thundered, large cumulus clouds of incense rose from the altar to the vault, and the monks, in their stalls with their hoods raised, didn't move a muscle. The congregation was uneasy. How can one hold the prayer book with frozen hands? How can one find some warmth? By adjusting one's coat as best as possible? Prosaic concerns took over.

In the afternoon, the Blessed Sacrament was exposed on the high altar. Several monks knelt on the sanctuary steps. Outside, the wind picked up. The silence in the abbey had the inflections of a snowstorm at the North Pole.

In the main courtyard, I found no living soul. No one dared to go out. Around five o'clock, the sun began to set. A low, pink light illuminated the countryside. A small vineyard worker's cottage, alone on the hill overlooking the monastery, appeared abandoned, and the muffled sound of the Creuse River passing through the monks' dam could be heard.

After dinner, in the darkness of the church, I saw the silhouette of Dom Forgeot walking slowly to the Nativity scene. He knelt to pray for a moment in front of the little manger where the baby Jesus slept. The cold was so intense that a kind of fog seemed to cover the back of the church.

On rainy days, the abbey church becomes humid. If a dry cold sets in, frost sticks on the stained-glass windows, making them resemble the mirrors at Versailles. In the darkness of the night, the building turns into a magical palace. The oldest monks remember when the holy water in the fonts turned into blocks of ice. The holy-water containers froze as well. For matins and lauds to be sung in the chapter house instead of the abbey church, the temperature inside must drop below four degrees. To move other services away from the abbey church, the mercury must dip below zero. In 2012, during Fontgombault's last severe winter, the church's thermometer remained at one degree for a week.

One day, the organist had asked for permission to rehearse a piece on the grand organ with a small electric heater by his side. After a while, the heater heated up enough, and the monk casually turned the device toward the organ woodwork. Lost in the passion of the musical movement, he didn't realize that the fine instrument didn't appreciate the process: its wood, exposed to the warm air, became charred. A passing monk in the church noticed it in time.

At the monastery, climate change is a tangible reality. The monks remember the winters when some of them would wear up to seven wool sweaters under their habits. That time has passed, but some monks still wear three or five layers of wool. For their part, the organists remember services where their fingers froze from the cold. Nowadays, they play comfortably. Each additional half-degree improves the musicians' comfort.

A passing Spanish monk at the abbey reportedly said when leaving, "I am happy to leave you with your novel refrigerator!" Another had formulated a fitting maxim: "Who withstands the cold of Fontgombault can withstand anything!" As for the priest of the neighboring parish, he affectionately calls the monastery church "the icebox"!

Nevertheless, even in this Siberian winter, all it took was to see the beautiful smile of a monk to understand that the cold meant little. There was frost, snow, and wind, but faith was greater, warmer, and more beautiful. Long live spring, though! Long live the sunshine of the beautiful days of May.

THE TIME OF CHERRIES

During the lockdown period caused by the coronavirus pandemic, the monks had closed the monastery's guesthouse. Dom Philippe was taking some rest. Usually, Holy Week is one of the busiest times of the year. In April 2020, the long corridor of rooms was empty; in the refectory, the guests' table seemed hopelessly lonely.

The abbey mobilized its farm to assist families in the region. Quantities of bread, eggs, cheeses; jars of jam and honey; and crates of apples left over were to be given to the poorest. The farm even donated a Jersey cow to provide meat to those who had none.

The beginning of spring was both joyful and sad. The April sun made it feel like summer. Fortunately for the farming brothers and gardeners, the rains were abundant; as Brother Raphael-Marie often said, "the best elements of good soil is rain and sunshine at the right time."

Before the feast of the Ascension, the three days of rogations were dedicated to imploring divine help. In the morning, after Mass, the monks went through the fields, orchards, and gardens to ask God for abundant harvests. The processions visited every corner of the monastery. The brothers even went the distance to bless the grain enclosures. The cows were astonished. They saw the long line of black-robed monks parading through the paths, censing, singing, and praying.

Nature was lush, and the farmer was happy. This year, there would be an abundant hay harvest. With the east wind, it would dry easily.

On the Creuse, Dom Pateau had undertaken major work on the power station. The work of modernization was so extensive that it was no longer clear whether they were controlling the great water of Marly or providing electrons to the poor monks. The entire community was passionate about the progress of the project. Trucks, excavators, and compactors constantly vied for the advantage. They even went so far as to build a cofferdam that crossed the river from side to side. The water current was strong and left little to tell.

In the kitchen, the cherries from the orchards arrived in large baskets. The harvest was early. In the cattle barns, the newborn calves frolicked. In the fields, cattle egrets and laughing gulls danced in front of Brother Raphael-Marie's tractor. When the tractor advanced, grasshoppers and insects of all kinds hopped around: the little birds just had to open their beaks to get the finest of lunches. On the monastery's lands, modern agricultural machinery promises a full stomach.

Behind the still somewhat cold walls of the abbey church, the organ breathed in the scents of the nearby orchard. The myriad fruit trees were nothing more than a large bouquet, where yellow, pale roses, and flax white dominated the gardens. Father Jorge, a monk of Argentine origin, practiced pieces by Johannes Brahms, Johann Sebastian Bach, Jakob Kortkamp, Lambert Chaumont, and Jehan Titelouze.

The notes of the Eighth Partita for Organ in C Minor, sublimated by the Latin American vivacity of the organist, sparkled with joy.

Fontgombault was still Fontgombault.

V
The Monks and the Bees

All the monks' work is wrapped up in a great whirlwind toward God. The abbot gives a homily, the brother tends to a bouquet of flowers, the cellarer writes a financial report, the gardener hoes a row of carrots; they all have equal importance. Each in his place and task, each in his toil under the gaze of the Highest.

A monk has no ambition. He does not claim equality. He must not be envious. In the *Rule*, Saint Benedict considers that "idleness is the enemy of the soul." The founder asks that the brothers engage in manual labor at certain times and at other times in the reading of the divine word, *lectio divina*.

Monastic happiness is the fruit of an ideal. Its supporting pillar has the simple name of prayer. Work is for God. The beauty of the liturgy is for God. The farm is for God. The infirmary is also for God.

The list of obediences — that is, of roles assigned by a superior — resembles an endless inventory. Discovering the long catalog of responsibilities, the layman widens his eyes. The bees have nothing left but to resume the organization of the hives. They almost appear as gentle anarchists compared to the unsinkable rigor of the monks.

One should be able to imagine how, behind the high enclosure walls, the monks work to make the abbey function. The respect for times for reading and prayer, the solemn celebration of the Divine Office, active participation in singing, the joy of walks and recreation, mutual obedience, and the spirit of service are not learned in a day. The monks in charge of training have an eminent role. The master of choir novices, the master of the lay brothers, the zelator of the choir novices — that is to say, the one who assists the master in the training of novices — the zelator of the lay brothers, the monk professors in charge of courses (in philosophy, liturgy, history of the Church, patrology, social doctrine of the Church, dogmatic theology, ecclesiology, mariology, moral theology, sacramental theology, canon law, Holy Scripture, and Latin) have the noble task of giving the younger ones the means of their monastic life.

We must also mention the chapter secretary, who keeps records for the vestures and professions as well as the charitable offices: confessors, the infirmarian and his assistants.

In the monastery, nothing is preferred to the work of God. Every day, more than twenty-five Masses are celebrated at Fontgombault. The monks responsible for everything related to the liturgy are legion. There is the sacristan and his assistants, who take care of the church cleaning, the material preparation of the offices with care for the cruets, the washing and ironing of liturgical linens; the *suce-mèche*, in charge of making and maintaining the candles; the monk responsible for devotional candles; the monk in charge of the conservation of art objects, the manufacture and repair of rosaries; the one in charge of the vestment workshop where liturgical ornaments are made and restored; the treasurer, who guards the monastery's relics; the *réglementaire*, responsible for all the monastery's bells and how to ring them, with his assistants, the second and the third *réglementaires*. (One can guess how cherished the bells are on the black riverbanks. They are called Maria-Petra, Michaëla, Joanna-Josepha, and Benedicta. The largest weighs about 1,600 kilos, the smallest, four hundred. They were blessed by Dom Roy on December 8, 1976.) We must not forget the monk in charge of managing Mass offerings, the librarian and his assistants, the bookbinders, and the monk responsible for choir books. Nor the monk in charge of maintaining the organs and the organists, the choirmaster, the precantor and the three cantors, the other members of the schola cantorum, the master of ceremonies, and his assistant.

And the inventory does not stop there! There are still the florists, with the monk in charge of the flower garden, the monk in charge of the church bouquets, the monks responsible for adorning the statues of Our Lady and Saint Joseph in the abbey. There are also all the charges related to the arts and crafts, workshops whose creations are either intended for worship or enhance daily life: the potter, the ceramicist, the monk responsible for enamels, the calligrapher.

Next come the tasks that ensure the material life of the monks and the abbey — works of first necessity, food, clothing, housing, cleanliness, and beauty of the place. Because, at Fontgombault, necessity goes hand in hand with gratuity. The cellarer oversees the monastery's economy, assisted by his accountant. The depositary, who has a say in everything that comes into the plates, with the first cooks — four brothers — the second cooks — eight brothers — the baker, the pastry chef, the butcher, the vintner-cellarman, the refectorian (in charge of setting the table), the monk responsible for peeling vegetables, the beekeeper, the confectioners — makers of jams, fruit pastes, and stuffed walnuts, a sweet specialty of the monks that visitors love — the farmer and his assistants, the brother who watches over the hens, the gardener and his assistants in the vegetable garden, as well as the orchard manager complete this beautiful picture.

There is also the chamberlain, in charge of what is necessary for daily life, from furniture to clothing, with his helpers in the laundry, the linen room, the tailor shop, both for the making of tunics and for linen repair, and cobbler shop.

Another string of responsibilities is associated with the maintenance of the abbey's buildings and equipment. In addition to the brother who is responsible and oversees everything, there are the plumber, painters, electrician, the monk working in the power plant and his assistant, who also have a say in heating, the IT specialist in charge of the entire network and video surveillance, the monk who controls the sound system in the church and refectory, the monk in charge of telephony, but also the monks' mechanics who maintain cars, tractors, the generator, bicycles, and they make everything work in the Benedictine factory!

For the lands that depend on the abbey, one monk oversees the exploitation of forest plots, another of the inner parks, another of the guesthouse gardens. After the specialized worker-monks, here are the heads of the corps of waters and forests.

We must also mention all the obediences related to relations with the outside world and arts and crafts intended for sale: the guestmaster and the second guestmaster, the father master of the oblates, the monk in charge of welcoming scouts, the chaplain who takes care of the unemployed and backpackers, the monks responsible for teaching children to pray, the porter, his assistants, and the two municipal councilors.

Finally, I conclude with the small printing house, the iconographers, the secretariat, the postmaster, and the archivist, who also keeps the chronicle wherein the daily life of the abbey is reported. In addition to the specific obediences, add the thousand and one services taken care of by one another — for example, each brother has an area of the house to clean — that allow the monastery to be maintained in peace, which is the tranquility of order, according to the beautiful expression of Saint Augustine.

"Each of the monks has a prominent role that the abbot gives him and that he must fulfill faithfully every day," summarizes Dom Pateau perfectly.

To govern the monastery, the abbot is assisted by the prior and the subprior. He also has a council. The number of its members depends on the size of the community. Currently, the council has five members. Two councilors, including the prior, are appointed directly by the abbot. The other three are elected by the chapter, composed of solemnly professed members of the choir. An absolute majority is required to be elected. Depending on the decisions to be made and according to the Constitutions of the Congregation of Solesmes, the abbot seeks the opinion or authorization of the council. For some acts, he asks the chapter for its approval; without this, he cannot proceed alone. Finally, he may sometimes turn to Dom Dupont, the abbot of Solesmes and president of the congregation, or to the Holy See.

These various councils are not intended to confiscate or limit the abbot's power, but rather to provide him with elements of a wise decision.

For matters concerning the monastery's services, the preparation of the council, or chapter consultation, obviously involves the person in charge, who may be asked to write a note sent to the councilors before the council meeting or even be present to explain the project and his point of view more precisely. It should be emphasized that the council is not limited to examining the project on a material or financial level; it is also responsible for considering the project's impact on the community's prayer life and its members.

Thus, the abbot, the council, and the chapter form three decision-making circles. But if the Church has provided that certain decisions require a vote in the council or chapter to prevent power abuses, mutual trust allows the three authorities to lean on one another rather than hinder one another.

The abbot must replace all the officers at least every three years. The great deposition is a decisive time in the monastery life. In the meantime, during a weekly conference, Dom Pateau may decide to relieve a monk of a particular obedience. Various reasons can lead him to do so. For example, Saint Benedict, in the chapter of his *Rule* dedicated to the monastery's artisans, invites them to practice their art "with all humility, provided the abbot allows it. But if one of them ever boasts of the knowledge he has of his craft, seeing that it brings something to the monastery, he will be relieved of his position."

The last general deposition took place in September 2019; Father Abbot had innovated by asking all the monks to write him a short note about their work and to add the name of one or more possible replacements they would consider taking their place. He wanted to remind everyone that obediences are never property.

The monk is poor. Nothing belongs to him. The common good of a monastic family is not the sum of each monk's own goods but rather the sum of everyone's renunciations. Happiness comes at this price. "Some days, when we go for a walk, some monks would like to stay at the monastery. But we must try for everyone's happiness to become everyone's happiness," Dom Pateau simply told me. Small individual jealousies, small fatigue, small fears must be sacrificed. This also applies to work.

Father Abbot announces the deposition of the charges with a handwritten message that he posts at the end of the break on the bulletin board. The monks discover it after none. The text is quite laconic: "7:05 p.m., deposition of charges." Everyone immediately understands that all the charges will fall at the end of the day.

In the evening, in the chapter hall, Father Abbot deposes the officers one by one — that is, the brothers in charge of an office but who do not necessarily have a commanding role toward the monks, unlike the deans in *Saint Benedict's Rule*. The prior, the subprior, the master of the choir novices, the master of the lay brothers, the cellarer, the first cantor, the chamberlain, the guestmaster, the porter, and the infirmarian have prepared an accusation where they report on the mistakes made in the exercise of their duties. The prior lost the community on a walk, causing a delay; he accuses himself. The infirmarian or the depositary made a slight mistake in the order of diets for older or sick monks; they accuse themselves. The first cantor misled the choir or harmed its unity; he accuses himself. The master of novices was not available enough to the novices; he accuses himself.

The prior and the subprior, who, by their office, are in the first place at the chapter, resume their former profession. They do the same in the refectory and the choir. On the cell doors, the names of the offices are replaced by the names of the monks. This usage may seem formal, but it still shows that no monk owns his office. The monk has only one wealth to preserve: God. He must never forget it. The *Rule* and the abbot take care to remind him.

At the end of this conference, the monastery must continue to live: the Divine Office must be ensured, the monks must be fed, the novices taken care of. Thus the abbot appoints substitutes to attend to daily activities pending the appointment of new officers and distributes the keys that the outgoing officers have returned to him.

Without delay, the abbot appoints a prior. The decision

is personal. As for all charges, he may reappoint the one who has just been deposed. In September 2019 he renewed Father Jean-Baptiste.

Once this is done, the abbot provides for the constitution of his council. In the case of Fontgombault, he appoints his second councilor, called *ex parte Abbatis*, and presides without voting in the election of the other three councilors by the chapter members. This election may have up to three rounds.

Can a monk change his obedience when he has been in office for a long time? Dom Jean knows that the work of explanation is crucial: "The brothers must understand that decisions are not made ad hominem. The greater good of the community, the good of the monk also, always takes precedence."

Benedictines make three vows: obedience, conversion of manners, and stability. Duration in an obedience should not lead the monk to consider himself immovable or authorize him to believe that only he can fulfill it. It takes courage and abandonment to give up an office after years, sometimes decades. The charge does not die with him; the monastery continues its path: "The brother will thank God for the gifts received during his service. He will even rejoice that another is in charge, doing his best to ensure a smooth transition. He will refrain from interfering in the affairs of his former office, either directly or indirectly." Dom Pateau's words may seem challenging. But the stability of the community structure comes at this price.

Once the council has been elected, Father Abbot convenes it and listens to it to prepare the "collation of charges." It is then decided on the new allocation of all obediences. These exchanges are sensitive because they directly impact the monks' lives.

An obedience should never harm a monk's prayer life. This is challenging for a cellarer, a guestmaster, an infirmarian, a porter. Other obediences, seemingly more innocuous, require emotional vigilance. For instance, the monk in charge of the chicken coop should not become too attached to the poultry he cares for. The farmer should not produce more milk than necessary. The beekeeper should not imagine that the bees of Fontgombault produce the best honey in France, even if that were true.

The abbot prefers an excess of prayer to an excess of work. The search for a constantly precarious balance is his daily bread. During the collation of charges in the chapter hall, Father Abbot officially announces the new assignments to the community. The substitutes return the keys, and the new holders receive them. We are reminded the Gospel's words: "I will give you the keys to the kingdom of heaven, and whatever you bind on earth shall be bound in heaven, and whatever you loose on earth shall be loosed in heaven" (Mt 16:19).

After a deposition, monks change cells, novices bid farewell to their former zelator, and monks leave instructions on the functioning of a charge they held until the day before. It is an emotional time. The new officer will not necessarily work the same way as his predecessor. But the latter must refrain from any criticism of how his successor handles things, and even from offering advice. He must now remain silent. Dom Pateau is a vigilant guardian, scrupulously adhering to this practice.

At the time of his appointment as prior, he remembers a text prepared for novices training. He was then the zelator of the choir novices. Except that he never delivered this lecture, as from one hour to the next, he was no longer the zelator.

The organization of Fontgombault is worthy of a Swiss watch. The abbot, representing Christ in the abbey, holds the complex mechanism in his hands. The monastery might seem to the eyes of the world as one of the last places where almost absolute power is exercised. Yet, fifteen centuries ago, Saint Benedict knew how to temper this power by reminding the abbot of the account he will have to render to God.

Would the monastery be a democracy, a society where

members exercise their sovereignty through the abbot and the councils they have elected, a government of monks, by monks, for monks? The answer to this question is no. The one who governs the monastery and the one for whom the monastery exists is not the assembly of monks; it is God. The monks, the council, the abbot have only one duty: to grasp God's will for the community, for each of its members, and to fulfill it.

VI
Quasi Modo Geniti Infantes[*]

In the *Rule*, Saint Benedict tells us:

> The abbot who has been judged worthy to rule the monastery must keep constantly before his eyes the name he bears and strive to fulfill by his conduct all the duties of a superior, for he is considered to hold the place of Jesus Christ among his brothers. This is why, with a mark of preeminence, he is given the name according to the apostle's words: 'You have received the Spirit of adoption of sons, whereby we cry: Abba, Father' (Rom 8:15). Thus the abbot should not teach, institute, or prescribe anything contrary to the precepts of the Lord, which God does not allow. Instead, his commands and his doctrine, like a spiritual leaven of divine justice, should

* "Like newborn infants" (see 1 Pt 2:2).

> spread and fill the hearts of his disciples.

At Fontgombault, the man who fulfills this daunting task has the face of a child, a teacher, a musician. This gentle man, who can become a wise man and a warrior, a lawyer, a judge, seems difficult to grasp, indefinable.

He could say to his monks, after the abbatial blessing: "Thus monastic life is a life made for children. Monastic life is a game, the great game of charity." Can we measure the strength needed to affirm such great realities with such simple words?

Jean Pateau was born June 9, 1966, in Les Sables-d'Olonne. After earning a physics degree at the age of twenty-two, a promising career lay ahead. He taught for two years in scientific preparatory classes at Lycée Stanislas in Paris, where he was the youngest teacher in the institution. However, he decided to pass through the austere gates of Fontgombault at the age of twenty-four. Ordained a priest in 1998, and becoming prior in 2004, he was elected abbot on August 18, 2011, at the age of forty-five, in the presence of the president of the Solesmes congregation, Dom Dupont. He succeeded Dom Antoine Forgeot. The task was not easy, but he faced it with great courage.

Dom Jean is an upright and sincere man, convinced that a good abbot is one who serves the monks of his community. With the even temper that characterizes him in every circumstance, he confided to me in one of our conversations:

> Saint Benedict emphasizes the "useful" nature of the abbot's service. This usefulness is not defined in relation to his person but in relation to God's plan for those whom the Lord has entrusted to him. The abbot must try to discern what this plan is and the path on which the monk must direct his life. But there is a difficulty: One must walk at God's pace; neither faster nor slower. The

> abbot remains a man. He would like to solve problems instantly, to run faster. But God may allow problems to last for years. Is it then a tragedy? No.

Only the divine pace matters. The word *auctoritas* comes from *augere*, which means "to increase." In a monastery, the exercise of authority aims at the good of the community and individuals. The abbot must help the monks to grow, which does not exclude some suffering on the part of both the one who obeys and the one who must command.

On the contrary, how to define a bad abbot? According to Dom Pateau, it would be a man centered on himself, sparing himself, not giving, keeping for himself, using the monastery and the monks for personal purposes. He would pontificate and not serve:

> The greatest joy of the abbot is to find God in the souls of his monks. When he sees the light of heaven in the hearts of his sons, he is happy. When the community is united, his joy is perfect. It takes a lifetime to make a good father abbot. If it is not God who builds the house, it is in vain that the workers labor. Heaven prepares the hearts of the abbots long before their abbatial blessings. The election is done by the vote of the monks who have a voice in the chapter, and the capitulants have the mission of discerning God's will for the community.

As surprising as it may seem, the vocation of the man who makes such assertions was a path strewn with thorns. His parents, deeply Christian, initially showed genuine opposition to his religious vocation. He discovered the Berry skies in his second year of high school. During a retreat at Fontgombault on Pentecost Monday in 1981, he was dazzled by the beauty of Gregorian chant. This stay remained engraved in his memory. Despite his father's pleas, imploring him not to enter the monastery, he eventually took the step, filled with great peace, certainty, and enthusiasm. A secret burned in his heart.

The first year, the parlors with his parents were difficult. His father remained silent, leaving his mother alone to address him. The pain overflowed. The times were tough. But turn of events did not lack surprises: Twenty years after his entry into the monastery, on his abbatial blessing, October 7, 2011, Dom Pateau's father returned to the abbey. The storms were memories of the past. Now he was happy. After experiencing serious heart and vascular problems, his presence was a miracle: Claude Pateau attended all the offices of that wonderful day.

Unfortunately, the new abbot lost his father a few weeks later. On the night of December 29, 2011, Dom Pateau was able to come and watch over him. Around five o'clock in the morning, Claude Pateau opened his eyes, seemed to get up as if to move toward something he saw, and departed. Very gently.

His son has always been sure of the meaning of his contemplative life. God would not abandon him: "The only pitfall is that I do not accept what the Lord gives me and asks of me by making the abbatial charge my own. We must not conform the things of life to our will. If I stay close to God, I have no fear."

Dom Pateau is not a man who doubts. Is it a form of radicality? In no way. He reflects a lot, sometimes changes course; he knows that difficult situations can arise. But he is certain that God is always present. In the life of faith, we should be able to continually question ourselves. The monk must ask himself if what he does is truly God's desire: "My vocation is something I have deeply embraced." But the pain did not remain an unknown land:

> It was a pain that I consciously provoked and accepted in my parents. I knew that God wanted me at Fontgom-

> bault. I had a certainty. In my family, the tear of physical separation gradually became great happiness, and for me, the pain revealed itself as certainty and tranquility. Nothing is impossible for God.

The monks of Fontgombault know that their abbot possesses a special grace to accompany and help troubled monks. Dom Jean's certainties help souls in pain to find the path of trust: "The day we arrive in heaven, we will understand the treasures of love that God has unfolded on each of our lives." These hours spent with the monks are happy moments for him.

You must watch Dom Jean walk. He doesn't seem to be coming toward you, and suddenly he's there. You think he's not looking at you, but he's scrutinizing you. He doesn't want to disturb anything, yet suddenly he intends to say everything. This will take as long as necessary; he will say what the truth requires. Dom Jean never takes half measures. He is not surprised by anything, without being an insensitive man. Things sadden him; then he goes to the front, like an intractable child. In the community, the abbot of Fontgombault can be fearsomely severe when it comes to breaches of fraternal charity. It makes him stubborn: "Breaches of charity hurt and kill community life. Monasteries rarely die of poverty; they die from lack of love in the hearts of the monks." The monastery must be "a laboratory of charity, a place of a love symphony, a conspiracy of mercy." He eloquently continues with the momentum of which he is capable: "It is not we who must live, but God who must take possession of the entire existence of the monastic community. Then, all of us will live."

One day, Dom Dysmas de Lassus, prior of the Grande-Chartreuse monastery, shared these words, which I have never forgotten: "God looks at the souls of the monks; he cares little about characters." Dom Pateau expresses it differently:

> Personalities evolve slowly in contact with the work God does in souls. Sometimes we may say: God has no discernment regarding the vocations he arouses in a monastery! Why did he allow this monk to come when daily life is difficult for him? But God has a plan. A father does not choose his monks. God alone chooses. Through the work accepted in the soul, the character will purify itself. God always draws man upward, to the ultimate encounter at the end of the road.

He remembers an old monk whose path was not easy, who at the end of his life confessed: "Oh, heaven will be so beautiful!" Dom Pateau adds: "God can only be good. He may correct harshly, but he remains good. In due time, his goodness triumphs and conquers the lukewarm heart and the cold intelligence."

Dom Jean is a mystic who does not reveal his cards. The flames of his goodness do not prevent him from maintaining a humble reserve. The man has his secret garden; he hides behind flashes that give the impression of a man of action. His intelligence is impressive. With his big round eyes, his gaze half childish, half judge of sorrows, his little arrows sometimes provocative, without the intention of causing harm, he advances and does not look back. He does not mince his words, which he chooses carefully:

> Ideology prevents us from listening to the silence of God. In a monastery, the tragedy occurs when there is a wall between God's plan and that of the monks. To understand God, one must show great forgetfulness of oneself. Evil consists in confusing the word of God with our desires. In a monastery, as in the Church, ideology is the tragedy, the false god, and the idol. Serving man and the monk implies taking him as he is. Reality is more

important than ideology. We must join the monk in the concreteness of his life, understand him to help him.

There is a bit of the spirit of the Society of Jesus in these words. And a form of resolute distance from all Jansenist hypocrisy. One thinks of the two standards of the *Exercises* of Saint Ignatius. A choice must be made: good or evil.

The abbot proposes to his monks to start from their life, their qualities, their wounds. How can one encourage the search for God in a monk while respecting his personality? His vocation is the encounter with heaven. The line is simple. Unfortunately, the fall is not impossible: "If the father abbot follows an ideology, he runs after his little personal method." He resembles a chicken without a head.

When a man enters the monastery, in his baggage he also carries his past, his passions, his political ideas, his family history. On the day of entry into the enclosure, there's no need to expect a miraculous break. Over time, the center of gravity of his personality shifts. Because the monk is fascinated by God, he is stretched toward him. The desire to enter the monastery betrays a deep call from God that will focus his entire new life. Passions, skills, and professions take a back seat.

I was thinking about Raïssa Maritain. At a certain point in her life, she sought to pray, she wanted to believe in God, but he had disappeared. Her friend Léon Bloy, to whom she confided, wisely replied: "Through science, you will only approach him. But it is through love that you will find him, and it is through this love that you will be happy and holy, for there is only one sadness, which is not to be saints."

Dom Pateau remembers his own journey: "Through science, I approached him. I got involved, and he took everything. He wanted everything. To let oneself be enlightened is to become blind."

In monastic life, the only thing necessary, sometimes distant and diffuse, becomes the sole, urgent necessity. Dom Pateau's voice becomes more passionate: "In the world, we know well that God is what really matters, but there are so many uninteresting things that captivate us. Over time, in the monastery, the light of God makes things that seemed unavoidable unnecessary."

The abbot of Fontgombault is fascinated by God: "God is dazzling. Look at nature. There is not a wonder that does not bear his mark. My past as a physicist, my astonishment at the universe, has always led me to him."

It is surprising to think that a human being has to be strange to become a monk. Monastic life is a leap into the void; upon arrival, one can find an unbearable desert, an illusory vocation, or an oasis, a place of joy. God attracts monks. They are owls hidden in the forests with their bewildered eyes, fascinated by the light.

How can one understand that a monk is no longer happy? Is his face sad? Does his presence at the Divine Office become superficial? Sometimes, he would like to be happy, but no longer believes he can. Father Abbot, with furrowed brows, answers my questions frankly:

> The gift to God and the gift to the brothers follow the same path. Monastic life is fragile. A monk stands between heaven and earth. One must have feet on the ground and head in heaven. Monastic life can put human nature to the test. But does the monk have the right to keep his sadness to himself?

One evening, I received this handwritten note from Dom Jean: "Dear Nicolas, during vespers, I was saying to myself that the moment when I am happiest is the sung office with my brothers. +Fr JP."

He came to provide some details to our conversation. I had

asked him to tell me about his best memory at the monastery. After a long reflection, he mentioned the jubilee day of Father Abbot Antoine, for his twenty-five years of abbacy. In 2002, all the daughterhouses of Fontgombault had gathered at the abbey. Monks from Randol, Triors, Gaussan, and Clear Creek had made the long journey to celebrate the anniversary of the dear father abbot: "The meeting of all the communities around Dom Antoine was wonderful." He added two personal moments: the day of his election as abbot and the time of reflection, the eve of his ordination, in the deserted church after compline, where he had remained alone for a long time in prayer.

There are also painful moments. The death of his first prior, Dom Yves Chauveau, remained a deep wound. The monk was carried away by a cardiovascular accident during a stay in Tuscany. On May 13, 2015, he was giving a lecture to the seminarians of Gricigliano.* The poor monk gave up his soul in a hospital in Florence a few weeks later, on July 2. He was buried in Fontgombault on July 9, in the presence of Cardinal André Vingt-Trois. A monk of exceptional stature, a brilliant professor and theologian, Dom Yves had been prior from 1977 to 2004, then from 2011 until his death. In his last months, he was tired. During his agony, Dom Jean kept hope, left Berry to visit him in Italy. On the day of his death, he felt profoundly alone:

> Despite our age difference, we understood each other spontaneously. I knew that God was taking away from me a holy monk, a close one, a prudent advisor. During his agony, I asked him to leave him to me. But his will was not mine. Sometimes, on his hospital bed, when he could no longer speak, Dom Yves pointed to the sky with his hand.

* This foundation of Fontgombault, in Tuscany, was transformed into a seminary for secular priests in the early 1990s. The connections with the French monks have always remained strong.

On the day of his burial, there was bright sunshine, and the sky was blue.

Dom Jean often thinks of Brother Clément. All his life he kept his position in the monastery kitchen, serving humbly, without ever complaining. He always smiled.

Father Henry, the former guestmaster, also remains in his memory. A man of letters, endowed with great culture and warmth, he was ill when Dom Pateau was elected, who opened up to him, and recounts:

> "How am I going to be able to write all the homilies and texts that an abbot must pronounce?" He looked at me knowingly and replied, "We will help you with that." A few months later, he died. He certainly knew that he would help me from his eternity.

Finally, Father Abbot spoke to me about Father Barais, a monk capable of radiating joy that did not come without real suffering. He was the sacristan, a difficult position. He worked tirelessly in the face of abundant demands. In a community, brothers who know how to give a small part of their happiness are important.

Suddenly, the abbot's voice became a prayer: "All the monks I have accompanied to death have left in great peace. When leaving Fontgombault, I hope that my soul will be similarly light."

What was the most important moment in the history of Fontgombault since the restoration of 1948? The question was important:

> Dom Édouard Roux planted the house on the banks of the Creuse. The orientation given later by Abbot Jean Roy was fundamental. The boat could have run aground. The headwinds were strong. In the seventies, he held the helm. Father Abbot Antoine took up the torch without

> ever getting discouraged. He was a driving force for unity. Liturgy was the struggle of his abbacy. He governed, he founded. We cannot swarm without being profoundly united. Dom Antoine had a grace of pacification. The future of the abbey is in God's hands. An abbot is nothing without his community. Fontgombault contributes its little stone to the history of Christian salvation. In the world, as a young student, filled by my stays at the abbey, I was convinced that there were only saints in this house of God. With the years, I know myself, I know my brothers. … No, there are not only saints. But all aspire to become one. The encounter with the truth of what we are is the first step on the difficult path of holiness. In this more just vision, the community paradoxically appears more beautiful to me, with its qualities, its joys, its faults, its lives. God helps us, under the gaze of Mary, who has a special presence in our walls.

Dom Jean Pateau is the father of a happy family, a family of monks.

I wrote that this man is indefinable. Now I can add, like all extraordinary people.

VII
The First Stirrings

A monk never forgets the day he understood that God was calling him. The morning of entering the cloister, the ceremony of perpetual profession, or the ordination Mass remain etched in his memory. But the day of recognition, the day of certainty of the call, is unique.

Father Ambroise remembers it very well. Coming from an aristocratic family, he entered the abbey at the age of thirty-one. Several of his uncles were priests; two were Assumptionists. A bright student, he attended the Prytanée Militaire de La Flèche. He discovered Fontgombault during a retreat. The young man was struck by the phrase written on the dusty sign at the back of the church: "The monks come seven times a day to give God the worship that is due to him."

We met on a rainy morning in a charming room in the guesthouse. Robust, with a youthful face, slightly flushed, he spoke to me about his previous work in real estate inspection. He lived in a house in the countryside with his hunting dog. A happy bachelor. His desire for independence was stronger than anything else. This son of a good family did not want to be enlisted. He wanted to be free.

In short, he was far from thinking about the vocation.

During the summer of 2008, he went to the monastery for a three-day retreat. The result was not very positive. For six months, he lost sleep. How could he talk about his torment that never left him? He returned to Fontgombault for another week of retreat and asked to meet a monk. The prior, Dom Pateau at that time, came to see him in his cell. But he declared himself unable to answer his questions. Dom Pateau promised to pray for him and sent him to the novice master.

In the morning, he wanted to become a monk. In the afternoon, he had doubts. In the evening, he knew nothing. Yet, deep down, he thought he was meant for Fontgombault. Then, at a specific moment, with lightninglike clarity, an unimaginable precision, he knew that he had to respond to God's call, feeling in a physical way that his religious vocation was irreversible.

It is difficult to enter the monastery at the age of thirty. For a year, once a month, Father Ambroise took the road to Berry. He sought to maintain contact, to keep the flame alive. He continued to keep his secret. His parents, brothers, and sisters knew nothing. One Sunday evening, in the kitchen of the family home, he decided to take the plunge and announce the big news. After the initial vertigo, like a leap into the void, his family accepted his choice. He had to quit his job. A colleague had this striking phrase: "I won't be able to say that it's good news, but it's big news."

How can one part with one's belongings at an age that is no longer that of prime youth? "It's sometimes crucifying!" The gift of his signet ring, to which he was attached, was not an easy gesture. A year later, learning that his father had modified the stock of his rifle to put it "to bed" saddened him. Monks, after all, are men.

The move did not happen without some tension, a touch of nervousness. He was torn away and released on the same day. "There is so much to unlearn," he confided discreetly — that is, the love of freedom, a form of selfishness, too.

When he came to Fontgombault, he was impressed by the monks' smiles. It was a deep and refreshing smile. This brightness reassured him about the reality of their happiness. He hoped for the same joy for himself. The serenity of the monks was a rock, an island to reach: "If they are joyful, then I can become joyful, too."

For Father Ambroise, the secret of the spiritual life is solely to love. The relationship with God is simple. The monk is a child who plays, and children who play are never alone. Either they play together, or they invent companions. The external world no longer exists for them.

What is the secret of this game? What is the rule? Nothing extraordinary: "The Lord is behind the door. He does not force. He waits for us to open it. He wants us to come spontaneously to him."

The day he entered Fontgombault, as his family left by car, no one spoke during the journey. His dear mother later told him: "We would have felt like we were breaking away from such a profound moment."

• • •

On the surface, Father Vincent's story is different, because he entered Fontgombault at the age of twenty-five. The young man was a soldier in the west of France where a beautiful fiancée was waiting for him. One summer day, he came to the abbey for a retreat to reflect on his upcoming marriage. His life was all mapped out. He had a job he loved, a fiancée he would marry soon.

In his family, no one had ever had a vocation. His decision, however, was sudden. In three days, he resolved to leave everything, settle all debts, and enter the monastery.

A few years earlier, he had stayed at the Benedictine abbey of Le Barroux. In the enchantment of the Provençal countryside, at the foot of Mont Ventoux, among olive trees and apricot trees, he did not feel a calling. During the three fiery days at Fontgombault, Dom Forgeot asked him to read Dom Delatte's text on vocation. These lines had a soothing effect. Yet, they were also hours of agony and sadness. In the refectory, he couldn't hold back his tears. As soon as the abbot saw him, without even speaking to him, he was certain that he had a monastic vocation.

He spent some time in another monastery to be sure of the abbey he should choose. "It must be understood that God calls in a specific place," he told me with his slightly mischievous, childlike gaze.

The novice master was not worried about his fiancée, but about his vocation. For his part, the young man did not wonder if the monastic life was for him. He simply thought, "If I don't open this door, I miss out on happiness." Yet, another promise awaited him. Within reach. Within reach of love. She had the face of a pretty young girl. But the desire for God shattered this momentum.

• • •

Even younger, with the eyes of a fiery adolescent, Father Athanase asked himself similar questions. His search lasted four years. He entered the monastery at the age of twenty-one, after a short year as a postulant in another community. Originally from western France, he earned a scientific baccalaureate, although he was more into literature. It was the pretentious time of the scientific baccalaureate. Then he entered the hypokhâgne (a first-year prepatory course for the arts), with the musical option, at Lycée Fénelon in Paris, where the headmistress, Marguerite Gentzbittel, who provided "an enriching but difficult education," reigned. There, between the four walls of his classroom, he understood that God was calling him.

How does this tall monk with a smiling face define his youth? "Working with the choir of the little singers and scouting had a decisive importance in my human and Christian formation," he said. Father Athanase was a rover scout. One winter evening, his scout leader asked him what he wanted to do with his life. In fact, he had a difficult time answering. The restless, somewhat nomadic young boy had so many projects that he could never have realized them in one lifetime: "In literary fields, no one knows what they want to do. I wasn't worried. But it's true that I had different desires every day." Without hesitation, the scout leader said to him, "Have you ever thought about becoming a monk?" The preparatory student was even more surprised because he had never set foot in a monastery. He vaguely knew that monks still existed. He imagined them lost in medieval mists.

The scout leader explained to him that he was thinking about the vocation for himself and shared a poorly made photocopy of the Burgundian abbey of Flavigny. "I was angry at such a way of dealing with my private life," Father Athanase said. "In the evening, I vaguely read the ugly sheet accompanied by an excerpt from the *Rule of Saint Benedict*. But I was so troubled that I slept poorly."

The next day, he couldn't follow the classes. He could only think of this improbable idea:

> I was nervous, worried. I felt that an unexpected and profound question had just imposed itself on me. At

> the end of the day, during the English class, at the back of the class, suddenly, I suddenly said to myself, "Why not!" I said yes to God in ten seconds. I didn't have any reason. In a moment, I was overwhelmed by immense and indescribable joy. I looked at the whole class, mostly composed of girls. My classmates were few who could say what they wanted to do. And I repeated to myself, proud as Artaban, "Me; now, I know." I didn't listen to a word of the last classes of the day. I knew nothing about monastic life, but I was happy. I had the vocation before talking about a monastery.

He called the scout leader and asked, "Where can we go to an abbey?" The reply was, "Go on a retreat to Fontgombault!" The February vacation was about to begin. He contacted the guest-master, and he arrived at the monastery for a week. In other words, for his whole life.

Upon arrival, it was freezing cold, and the countryside was asleep in a white coat. The church temperature did not exceed two degrees. The hypokhâgneux was impressed by the forty hours. The monks use this term to denote an earnest supplication in which they implore God, taking turns in the adoration of the Blessed Sacrament exposed with solemnity for forty hours. This long prayer takes place in the days preceding the start of Lent, from Quinquagesima Sunday to the famous Mardi Gras. In Father Athanase's dazzling memory, the monks processed around a church petrified by frost. Clad in ample black habits, they each held a candle. And they sang.

He did not think of making a tour of France's monasteries. He instinctively knew that if he became a monk, his choice would be Fontgombault: "Vocation is not a choice between several possibilities but assent to God's choice. God decides. We only have to say yes or no. The choice is already made. It's a loving call."

After the preparatory class, he enrolled at the Sorbonne in classical literature, just to pass the time: "I always wanted to enter the monastery. After a year in another monastic family, I returned to Fontgombault in 1994. My aspirations were there."

Comparing the overactive Parisian life and the carefully measured hours of Fontgombault, the first months in the monastery were tumultuous. Initially, the lack of physical exertion was difficult, insurmountable. In the novitiate, life is regulated, the young monk has only an hour and fifteen minutes for daily tasks and physical exercise: "But when you have to fold sheets, you're not necessarily outside. Sometimes, the novice master allowed me to run in the woods before matins, in the middle of the night. I absolutely had to expend energy."

The novitiate is like the discovery of a new world. Father Athanase has kept precise memories of these extraordinary moments: "I was captivated by the joy that existed in the enclosure. This happiness was inconceivable from the outside. The atmosphere of recess seemed light, magnificently simple. The youngest and the oldest monks are all children."

Why this joy? Does the monastic life's balance, the regularity of prayer, and the childlike status in which monks float allow them to abandon difficulties, fears, and anxieties? In an abbey, duty is a categorical imperative. The monk knows what he must do and when he can do it: "One always feels like going back home, like a student returning home. Parents take care of everything. It's a reassuring world."

Initial euphoria is not fake. But this security has a price. It exists only in proportion to the abandonments consented to by the monk. He is faced with a choice: either he rebuilds in the secrecy of the enclosure what he has abandoned by trying to preserve his preferences, his time, his habits, and the problems return; or he continues to abandon himself and reaps a hundredfold. The fight never ends. The more the monk abandons himself, the more he becomes like a child — light, serene, and free.

In a monastery, one can take on a thousand difficulties to avoid leaving behind one's previous life. The monk who makes this choice is not easily identifiable. The abbot remains the vigilant guardian of the lighthouse. He knows the color of the storms on the horizon.

In my conversations with Father Athanase, I sometimes felt like I was hearing a romantic hero, dressed in a black tunic. But my interlocutor was very serious:

> Everything I learned in my youth served the monastery. Nothing was in vain. Latin, singing, and scientific studies were useful to me. Providence helped me. I would have liked to be a doctor, engineer, lawyer, composer, journalist, writer. The only way to realize my dreams was to enter Fontgombault. By renouncing all my fantasies, I realized them all. When I have to perform an obedience, I choose to love it. I don't know how to resist.

• • •

Monastic joy is like Gregorian chant. It is light, it flows, it enchants. Nothing can be dramatic. The child who loses a game is sad. But he immediately starts running again. At home, parents are there.

Brother Norbert may perhaps resemble this child for his entire life. When he entered the abbey on August 15, 2010, he was thought to be fifteen years old, although he was ten years older than that. A decade later, he has not changed much.

Previously, he had spent two years in an apostolic religious community. The experience was happy, but he gradually realized that he wanted to embrace a contemplative life. He grew up in the Paris region in a large family. As a scout, he came to Fontgombault for camps. The young man also sometimes took the path to the abbey to study for exams. He knew the place well.

In his senior year, at nineteen, he became certain that he had a vocation: "God touched my heart in a definitive way. I often had trouble deciding. But the will to respond to the call of heaven was overwhelming. There were still six years between my response and entry into Fontgombault."

It was during a retreat in the Berry abbey that a second decisive call was heard "The good Lord laid his hand on me. I wanted to stay with the monks," he explained. "In my journey, there was a desire for perfection through charity. I understood that monastic life would allow me to respond to it absolutely. I was sure of myself. I wanted to embrace Benedictine life."

Not without sadness, he had to leave his ties; Fontgombault was the real port. Everyone knew he wasn't leaving out of cowardice.

According to Benedictine tradition, he could no longer see his family during the vacation period. He accepted this sacrifice of the contemplatives. The arrival was magnificent. He felt like joining the cohort of all the monks who had committed themselves for fifteen hundred years in the wake of Saint Benedict: "I immediately wanted this heritage to be existential. I had to receive and live. I was filled with great peace. Liturgical life filled me with joy. Over time, we realize how delicately God leads us."

Brother Norbert was fascinated by the repeated calls of God throughout the monks' lives: "The bell that rings to summon the community to the offices expresses the same call to serve and praise God." He wants to continue, search, and cultivate the peace that heaven gave him at Fontgombault.

Despite a small trial, he never doubted again: "You must not look back on yourself. The only necessary thing is at this price."

For a monk, anxiety is the consequence of dispersion among multiple things:

> On the contrary, peace simply comes from the rediscovered and maintained friendship with God. In the world, we must constantly deepen the friendship we have for our loved ones. It is the same with God. The monk remains a weak man. He stumbles constantly. But he gets up. In a monastery, one can guess what the intimate life with God in paradise will be like.

If you listen to Brother Norbert, you know that the statement of St. Theodore then Studite is true: "A monk is one who directs his gaze toward God alone, who leaps in desire toward God alone, who is attached to God alone, who chooses to serve God alone, and who, in possession of peace with God, becomes a cause of peace for others."

A monk is one who loved one world but preferred another, one that is smaller, more fragile, madder.

During our exchanges, I often thought of another monk. Above all, this one loved his family, the navy, water, and the open sea. One day, he entered Fontgombault: "I have never seen the sea again. When I flew over the Crozon Peninsula and the Saint-Guénolé Abbey of Landévennec by helicopter, I looked at the monastery and thought that the monks were praying. But I didn't think of anything specific for myself." From up there, he had a kind of intuition of heaven; now, he says with nostalgia, the land sickness is more persistent and tenacious than seasickness or air sickness. Thinking back to his former life as a sailor and helicopter pilot, he quoted aviator Jean Mermoz: "I would never want to come down again." In Berry, there is no large horizon. The Lord calls for something else.

A sailor's life is the open sea, infinite spaces. A monk's life is the infinite, it is God.

VIII
The Magnificent Memory of Father Abbot Antoine*

He possessed the unwavering regularity of great workers. When the monks came to see him in his office, they invariably found Father Abbot with a pen in hand. A lecture, a sermon, a meditation, a letter: He wrote continuously.

At the time of this profile, Dom Antoine was taking care of the minor cleaning tasks in the area dedicated to Our Lady of a Good Death. The task involves daily cleaning of the burners at the base of the Romanesque statue. At eighty-seven years old, morning and evening he comes with his broom and his humble tools to tidy up the forest of candles and brush off the cooled

* Dom Antoine Forgeot passed away on Saturday, August 15, 2020, just a few hours after the feast of the Assumption Mass. I didn't want to change this portrait: These pages will forever remain the ones he read a month before his departure for eternity.

wax that has spilled. With a stooped back and a limping gait, he faithfully fulfills his last obedience.

Dom Antoine Forgeot was born October 15, 1933, in Bayonne. After a year of studying law at the Catholic University of Paris, he entered the cloister on October 8, 1953. His older brother, Xavier, had preceded him and was a novice then. He made a simple profession in 1955 and left five days later for military service in the health services, in Montauban and later at Val-de-Grâce, returning in 1957. During this period, he lost his brother, who died suddenly of a stroke. He completed his novitiate in 1959 and made solemn profession in 1960. He was ordained a priest in 1964 and earned a bachelor's degree in theology in 1966. Responsibilities followed: He was appointed zelator for the choir novices by Dom Roy in 1966, novice master in 1971, and then prior in July 1976. Unfortunately, on September 23, 1977, in Rome, during a congress of abbots, Dom Roy was struck by a sudden heart attack.

That dark day marked a break, a tipping point for the entire community. The young prior had never fully imagined that he would one day succeed his dear Father Abbot. Dom Forgeot took on the delicate task of organizing the funeral: "It was a painful ordeal. We had to arrange for the repatriation of the body, which returned to Fontgombault on September 27, stopping at Gricigliano [seminary] and Randol [Abbey], the young foundations." The procession arrived just after the Conventual Mass. All the monks were gathered. The remains solemnly crossed the abbey church and paused in front of Our Lady of a Good Death.

A few days later, he was elected father abbot. His abbacy lasted three long decades — intense, beautiful, and fruitful years. No one imagined that he would one day resign from his position. Yet, in the summer of 2011, after a discussion with Dom Dupont and two monks from the abbey, he announced his resignation.

It's not easy to understand the former abbot. At first glance,

Dom Forgeot seems distant, almost hieratic. Yet, he knows how to be approachable, smiling, and considerate.

He was primarily a man of heritage. He believed in the precious legacy of Dom Roy. So he fought. The storm threatened to sweep everything away, but he held on. Dom Forgeot did not yield an inch of ground. He may have seemed to retreat, but in truth he stood firm like an ageless oak. In the seventies and eighties, the liturgical crisis raged. It divided, angered, and buttressed. In 1969, Solesmes adopted the new Missal of Paul VI; Fontgombault followed five years later, which felt like an eternity. But the monks of Berry wanted to return to the old rite of John XXIII. "My predecessor knew that the liturgy is the path of the soul to God," explained Dom Forgeot. "He had plowed the furrow. It remained for me to follow his teaching. I had to be faithful. I had nothing to change."

The battle for the liturgy truly reflects Dom Forgeot's iron will. Stories, whispered in hushed tones, tell even more about his strong character. One day, a visitor expressed surprise at the winter cold in the abbey church. Dom Forgeot's response came on time, relentless: "No one has ever died from it!"

On October 12, 1952, he stayed at Fontgombault for the first time. He accompanied his brother Xavier, who was entering the cloister. After lunch, they walked as a family. The superior of Fontgombault, Dom Roux, walked with his father, and the two Forgeot brothers followed at a short distance. Antoine Forgeot thought that Dom Roux was already old, although he was only fifty-seven. But his admiration was instantaneous.

He returned for a retreat in August 1953. Approaching his twentieth birthday, he was sure of his vocation. On October 6 of the same year, he definitively unpacked his suitcase at the abbey. The next day, on Dom Roux's abbatial blessing, Fontgombault was in celebration. The famous choirmaster of Solesmes, Dom Gajard, had come especially to prepare and direct the monks' chant. Then, on October 8, the younger Forgeot crossed the threshold of the cloister. Dom Antoine still remembers that they celebrated the Conventual Mass for the deceased of the order and the benefactors. At that time, he did not know the customs he would one day be the guardian of.

Like all young novices, he was a bit lost. His brother Xavier was designated to be his guardian angel. Before the trip to Berry, he had visited the Basque Abbey of Belloc. During his military service, he had visited the monasteries of En-Calcat, Tournay, and Saint-Benoît-sur-Loire. But God wanted him at Fontgombault.

Dom Forgeot has excellent novitiate memories. At that time, the abbot was also father master. Dom Roux's lectures for the novices, given three times a week, enchanted him. His favorite class was the one dedicated to the holy *Rule*: "It's truly the professional training of the monk." He uttered these astonishing words with the utmost seriousness.

The words of Dom Antoine are rare. One must observe him closely to understand him better; to understand his silences and what union with God can mean. Lives of fidelity, humble lives, simplified lives shape gazes, voices, and breaths. Dom Antoine Forgeot is of this rare lineage.

In some monasteries, the retiring abbot is asked to leave his abbey. In Dom Forgeot's case, the question was raised on the day of his successor's election. Dom Pateau still remembers: "My freedom with regard to Father Abbot Antoine meant that I did not deem it necessary. I have never regretted that decision. Father Abbot went to Clear Creek for a few weeks to give me time to take charge of the abbey. Things were done very simply."

The emeritus abbot has a clear vision of the final stage of monastic lives:

The old monk must strive to be discreet, in the simplici-

> ty of truth. He is obliged to be as unobtrusive as possible. Above all, he avoids the temptation of marginalization, more or less conscious, in relation to a community that he may have difficulty keeping up with due to the limits or fragilities of age.

Dom Antoine knows that he is approaching the end of his earthly existence. He often coughs. His gaze sometimes wanders. His gait is less assured. On walks, he always takes his cane.

The monks split into small groups. At the forefront is often Dom Pateau. The oldest bring up the rear. Dom Forgeot is among them. Recently, for the first time, he organized a major cleanup in his office. He arranged, tidied, burned:

> There is a state of grace for every moment. The grace that accompanied me when I was a young novice is not the same as the one helping me be an old monk. As abbot, I had to face many difficulties, especially with the new foundations. I was not alone. God, through the assistance of his grace, helped me. Today, I am reduced to almost nothing. God always remains with me. If we try to be faithful, he gives us what we need for the current mission at every moment. God now allows me to accept the passing of time and to live simply.

In chapter sixty-eight of the *Rule*, Saint Benedict writes:

> A brother may be assigned a burdensome task or something he cannot do. If so, he should, with complete gentleness and obedience, accept the order given him. Should he see, however, that the weight of the burden is altogether too much for his strength, then he should choose the appropriate moment and explain patiently to

> his superior the reasons why he cannot perform the task. This he ought to do without pride, obstinacy, or refusal. If after the explanation the superior is still determined to hold to his original order, then the junior must recognize that this is best for him. Trusting in God's help, he must in love obey.

Dom Forgeot likes to talk about obedience in Benedictine life. For a long time, the monks submitted to his judgment. Now, he listens and obeys his successor himself.

Sometimes, during our meetings, there was an enigmatic silence. Dom Forgeot has nothing to hide. Perhaps he prefers perfecting his silence rather than professing additional opinions that he deems unnecessary? He listens more than he speaks, yet this doesn't prevent him from having decisive judgments. The former abbot that he was still pierces under the weight of the years. One cannot have been the superior of Fontgombault for so long without some enduring habits.

One imagines that he keeps his best words for his beloved successor. Imagine some advice given in a low voice. Imagine the seriousness of Dom Jean. He must then be both a son and a father.

How does the monk accept old age? When I asked him this question, he answered without hesitation. His voice was low, a bit raspy:

> When one does not die young, one must resign oneself to becoming an old man! We must not view old age as a sad or demeaning final stage. It belongs to God's plan. The monk, and every man, can age happily. Death is a moment, a threshold to cross. An old man knows that he is constantly approaching this threshold. We do not know what is behind the door. But we know that they

> open toward God. Monks have only one thing to do: We must prepare ourselves as best as possible to be in the best state. I strive to be ready.

The old monk brings much to his abbey. He remains present; that is important. His fidelity encourages the younger ones. The community can benefit from his beautiful experience. He is the memory of the monastery: "At Fontgombault, I must transmit the memories that I am the last to know."

Fidelity remains a struggle. Until the last days of a monk's life, one must never abandon observance: "It's easy to settle into half-measures. A monk who recovers from an illness must resume his habits as quickly as possible. The abbot judges what each one can or cannot do."

It is not just about transmitting great principles. During recreation, Dom Forgeot can recall small events, old conversations, witty remarks, and anecdotes that the younger ones are unaware of. Old monks should not take themselves too seriously. They should not pose as wise. There is no room for any form of veneration. The old must love the young, and the young must revere the elders.

Dom Forgeot often thinks about the judgment of God:

> We must not imagine judgment as a tribunal. It is the soul that judges itself. At the threshold of eternity, the soul sees the wonder of God and understands if it is ready or not to join him. It goes of its own accord to purgatory or, unfortunately, to hell. In these moments, the protection of the holy Virgin is very important.

In the *Rule*, Saint Benedict teaches his monks that they must "have death before their eyes every day." The thought of eternal life is not only for monks approaching the end. Novices are not exempt from such activity. Eternity begins in the life of faith. What will eternal life be like? When I asked him this question, Dom Forgeot's words became poetic: "The vision of God. Perfect happiness. New heavens. The saints await us."

Despite mystical concerns, the former abbot rarely loses his restrained humor:

> Dom Roy and Dom Roux will help me pass through the door. We forget too much the words of Saint Benedict who asks us to "fear hell." God is all mercy, and all justice. Sister Faustina, however, says that what offends God the most are people who doubt his mercy. The thought of heaven should arouse the desire to go there. In the novitiate, Dom Roux used to say: "I do not know if we will have manual work in heaven. But if we do, we will practice it like a sport."

Dom Forgeot speaks with joy about the abbots of Fontgombault. On the one hand, he venerates his two predecessors as saints. On the other hand, if asked to summarize his successor in one word, he says, "Wonderful." He sees the qualities in him: "Our abbot is a very good theologian, he has a beautiful authority, he shows true charity, and everyone knows he is an extraordinary technician." It is true that the transition from one abbacy to the other was exemplary.

Between Dom Roy and Dom Pateau, he sees himself as a transitional abbot. At most, he concedes that the interlude was long: "I was the little instrument that God used for a long time. If we know that we have become an instrument in God's hand, we must strive to be as malleable as possible. Dom Roy had drawn a straight line. I followed it."

Sometimes, surreptitiously, the adamant Dom Forgeot becomes a child again. He has the eyes for it. The soft voice, the breath, the timidity too. In these moments, he opens up more easily: "Time runs fast, and that's good. Here below, we are in exile. I didn't see my sixty-seven years in Fontgombault go by. I have some reference points. Nothing more. The years of novitiate and those of studies seem a bit long. Before ordination, the destination is precise. After that, the goal is heaven." Time flies like clouds, the "wonderful clouds," as the poet Charles Baudelaire would have said.

Despite his modesty, he dares to make a small confession: "When we age, many memories of childhood come back. I rediscover moments and faces that I had forgotten. It's very pleasant. One day, a visitor asked Marthe Robin* what she would do in heaven. She answered without hesitation: 'I will gambol.' With age, we already gambol a little."

Seriousness returns fast, accompanied by new enlightening words: "The old monk needs to be on his knees before his abbot. Like a novice entering the monastery."

Sometimes, I would tnotice that time was definitely a bit mischievous on the banks of the Creuse. It did not pass ... When I asked Dom Forgeot, he agreed: "Fundamentally, nothing has changed. We are still what we received from Dom Édouard Roux. He himself was the son of the great abbots of Solesmes."

Nothing has changed, and Dom Forgeot reluctantly speaks of his achievements. He says in a low voice that the community has remained fervent and faithful. It is agreed that unity has never been lacking; this unity also prevails among the daughter-houses of Fontgombault.

Dom Forgeot completed the launch of the abbey in Randol, opened Triors in Drôme, and Donezan in Ariège, then wholeheartedly embarked on the adventure of Clear Creek in the United States. Thirteen members left Fontgombault for the

* Marthe Robin (1902–81) was a mystic, confined to her small family farm in Drôme, who experienced numerous visions.

distant location of Oklahoma, United States. This heroic launch left a lasting impression. Dom Forgeot returned there one last time in 2011. The sixty American monks of Clear Creek are now preparing for their own foundation.

The demanding wisdom of Dom Forgeot never kept him far from his monks. But what is important is humility. Paradoxically, it is dazzling. It surpasses everything.

Charles Péguy marveled: "What astonishes me, says God, is hope. And I cannot get over it. This little hope that seems like nothing at all. This little girl, hope. Immortal."* How many times have I thought of these verses while listening, observing Dom Antoine Forgeot? Often, I repeated the verses to myself.

On July 16, 2011, Dom Forgeot resigned. His resignation was carefully considered. He regretted nothing, had no doubts; Dom Jean would be the perfect successor. One day, he had no more responsibilities. He only acknowledges that he "felt lighter." Each day of his abbacy was ordained because he had left nothing to chance. He had no merit, he thinks; God decided everything.

Why this persistent desire to imagine that he was not much? That his usefulness was minimal? I will probably never have the answer.

Dom Antoine would have been a pilgrim with a slow pace. Now, he looks at the future with serenity. He has confidence. In the evening, after the office of compline, he prays near the graves of his predecessors. One day, his body will rest in this soil.

In 2008, at the Collège des Bernardins, Benedict XVI dedicated a significant speech to the origins of Western monasticism. He stated:

> Amid the confusion of these times, when nothing seemed to resist, the monks desired the most important thing: to apply themselves to find what is valuable and

* Charles Péguy, *The portico of the mystery of the second virtue*, Paris, Émile- Paul, 1911.

> always remains, to find life itself. They were in search of God. They wanted to move from the inessential to the essential, to what alone is truly important and certain. It is said that their being was oriented toward eschatology. But this must not be understood in the chronological sense of the term — as if they lived with their eyes turned toward the end of the world or toward their own death — but in the existential sense: behind the provisional, they sought the definitive.[†]

Reading these lines, I inevitably think of Dom Forgeot, the sense he wanted to give to monastic life, to its stability.

Two memories, two images of the former abbot of Fontgombault will always remain in my memory.

It was the summer of 2019. It was very hot. After lunch, the second guestmaster, Father José-Marie, took a few guests to visit the abbey. I knew the places well. But I was happy to join the small cohort. The young monk presented the abbey to us with great erudition. The retreatants were focused. The harsh June light splashed the sanctuary. Suddenly, at the turn of the ambulatory, I saw Dom Forgeot. He was kneeling in prayer in an axial chapel. The former abbot was surrounded by a few elderly monks. He had placed his glasses beside him, and his hands hid his face. He seemed tired and full of great spiritual strength.

The guests admired the columns, the volumes, the light. But the gaze had to turn away from the stones to rest for a few brief seconds on Dom Forgeot. For in that moment, there was nothing more estimable than the humble prayer of a monk who would soon leave this world.

I will also remember an uneventful winter day. This particular morning in January 2020, Father Abbot was absent. At lunch,

† Benedict XVI, "To the World of Culture," a speech delivered at the Collège des Bernardins in Paris on September 12, 2008.

Dom Forgeot found himself alone at the abbatial table. Suddenly, his small hoarse voice resonated under the great vaults. He began the recitation of grace. In these unchanging moments, silence is the rule. But on that day, the silence was unique, sublime, celestial. Because, without realizing it, the silence was shaped, transformed by a single presence: his.

In the evening, during the reading of the traditional passage from the *Rule*, Dom Forgeot was again alone at his table. During the reading, he resembled an old emperor, stoic, impeccable. The scene was fascinating. The fragile body upright, the head deeply inclined, the eyes half-closed, he was the perfect image of the wise man, the beloved father, the one in prayer.

IX
Looking Through Albums of the Past

The albums were placed on the table in the library. In the past, all families took care to create these lovely books that contained so many memories. Births, baptisms, first Communions, birthdays, weddings, celebrations, and travels passed by so quickly. In the abbey as well, photographs are conscientiously tucked into their corners; handwritten comments accompany all the snapshots.

I was looking at these images of another time with Dom Antoine Forgeot. He hadn't turned the pages in a long time. The monk is not a *homo nostalgicus* ("nostalgic man"). The past matters little to him; the future does not worry him. He lives fully in the present. For he awaits eternity.

The most venerable images showed the arrival of the monks

in Berry. We followed the colony of twenty-three Benedictines from Solesmes settling into the large empty buildings. An abbey is a family. Flipping through these pages, I felt like spending a joyful moment with the august grandfather of Fontgombault. The memory of the former abbot was impressive. It sometimes played little tricks on him. Nevertheless, the old monk would have made more than one person blush.

"Everything must change so that nothing changes"* is a phrase of the Sicilian writer Giuseppe Tomasi di Lampedusa applied wonderfully to our conversation. Generations of monks passed, personal stories and or journeys were different, but, in truth, nothing had changed since 1948. From album to album, the faces were the same. The smiles, the looks, the gestures, too.

We spent long hours examining the album dedicated to the life of Dom Édouard Roux, abbot of Fontgombault from 1948 to 1962, the year of his death. The photos of the Marseille childhood of the little boy born in 1896, the wise adolescent, the young soldier gave way to the angelic, happy, and lively young monk, who first entered the British Quarr Abbey before joining Solesmes with his brothers after World War I.

The man had a fiery temperament, and he had never recovered from a terrible appendix operation performed without anesthesia. This little barbarity had weakened his health. At that time, driven by a law of July 1, 1901, hostile to congregations, the Benedictines had left Solesmes for England in September of the same year. In the photos of this forced exile, Dom Forgeot did not recognize everyone. He searched deep in his memory but could not put a name to the faces of those bygone days. Sometimes, he amused himself: "Well, who is this monk smiling at the angels? And this one, he is all round! I don't recognize him."

Dom Roux had a stern, icy, almost severe expression, but beneath the face hid a just man. Sensitive and modest, he un-

* Giuseppe Tomasi di Lampedusa, *The Leopard* (Milan: Feltrinelli, 1991), 44.

derstood his world. The album reproduced excerpts from the countless affectionate letters that the monk sent to young novices during the period of turmoil in the colonial empire, from Indochina to Algeria. Dom Forgeot, for example, left on August 17, 1955; he returned November 1, 1957. Sometimes, during the same period, two or three novices were far from Fontgombault. Here are some excerpts from the preserved letters. To Pierre Rotgé, he wrote on April 22, 1954: "The future belongs to God; let's not think too much about it. The present is so beautiful, wherever we are, since heaven is in our souls, and everywhere we adore in spirit and in action." On April 28, 1954: "The program is not the same for everyone. The essential thing is to live yours in love."

To Antoine Forgeot, on August 24, 1955: "It is so simple to give everything, and it should also be simple not to cease doing it as the days pass one by one in various ways." On February 21, 1957: "All trials have a meaning, a purpose, an end. Blessed are the souls who know how to discover them and who find in suffering a nourishment for deeper faith and more absolute love." On August 8, 1957: "The weather is heavy, very hot. This does not prevent being happy and saying foolish things to the Lord: *quoniam bonus* ['for he is good']."

To Xavier Forgeot, the older brother, on November 18, 1954: I leave you in the arms of Our Lady, those arms that carried Jesus as a child and dying." On January 21, 1955: "You could be at the North Pole, [and] we would not be separated. Distance does not play for souls that are spirits and find themselves in God whom they adore in spirit and in truth." On August 21, 1956: "God alone is interesting, and everything else is nothing. How one should know how to do without everything; live in that poverty that is wealth: *dives et pauper* ['rich and poor']."

To Jean-Yves de Lamarzelle, on August 6, 1961: "You can count on me who give my life for you, but my days are numbered. You will love my successor even more, whoever he may be." On February 8, 1962: "Divine tenderness envelopes everything, and above all, the hour of death." On February 15, 1962: "Everything has an end on this earth, thank God! But eternal life will not, thank God a thousand times!"

In the beautiful shots of his life, the man from Marseille appeared alternately as a kind young monk; a dreamy, determined, feverish, or worried religious. We followed him with his novices at Solesmes, he who was a beloved and admired master. We scrutinized the meticulous preparation for Corpus Christi in the French gardens of the mother abbey, the conversations with Dom Germain Cozien, the third successor of Dom Guéranger. Our eyes stopped on a first walk on the banks of the Creuse. On the other hand, Dom Antoine did not remember the impressive images of the restoration work on the choir of the Berry church. At the time, Dom Roux had decided to dismantle the great rood screen. I lingered on the photograph of a recreation in 1953, near the apse, the solemn and glorious day of the abbatial blessing, in the presence of the future Cardinal Joseph-Charles Lefèbvre, archbishop of Bourges, and Dom Cozien; Dom Roux spoke with a prelate, and Dom Dupriez, from the abbey of Hautecombe, conversed with Prince Xavier de Bourbon-Parma, in front of the sacristy. A vanished world.

In those days, an abbot had to pose for his official portrait. The image was hieratic and cold. Today, it would not be the same. The Benedictines then wore the tonsure. Then came a group photo at Solesmes, dating from May 1948.

Dom Forgeot obstinately searched for Dom Joseph Gajard. We finally found him. The musician wore rimmed glasses that betrayed long-standing myopia. They were 110 monks at that time. Dom Forgeot's slender fingers passed from face to face. This one was a great artist, that one a recognized intellectual, another an excellent gardener; he remembered everyone's talents. Suddenly, the light declined. A November shower fell on

Fontgombault. You could not see much anymore. We had to light a pretty desk lamp to continue our journey into the past.

We stopped at a photograph taken near the abbey chevet (eastern end of the church). Dom Forgeot looked long at Father Isambert, who died in the prime of life. A few moments later, he told me about little Brother François, a monk who had not taken vows but died in the odor of sanctity.

In the last years, the features of Abbot Roux had become painful. The smile was noble, fraternal, but the eyes that sunk into the sockets betrayed a form of physical collapse. The man was exhausted; he had given much.

In February 1962, returning from Paris, Dom Roux had stopped at Chartres Cathedral. After celebrating Mass, he remained on his knees for two hours in front of the statue of Our Lady of the Pillar. The monks later learned that he had asked the Mother of Christ to call him back to heaven.

A few weeks before his death, he had gone to bless a mission cross in a nearby village. It was bitterly cold, and the abbot contracted pneumonia. His agony was painful, breathing became difficult. On March 19, 1962, Dom Édouard Roux left his dear sons.

Curiously, a monk had taken numerous images of Dom Roux a few hours after his passing. About fifteen shots showed him lying on a bed covered with a black sheet, or in his coffin placed on the floor, near the cathedra. The photographer hadn't missed anything. We turned pages and pages. The face of the deceased had transformed. Despite his translucent complexion, he seemed pacified and serene. The ascetic prince had certainly found his King.

The funeral of Dom Roux was beautiful. One could see the long procession leaving the chapter room, passing through the courtyard of the guesthouse, and climbing the steps of the royal porch of the abbey church. The photos in an album titled *Fu-*

neral of Father Abbot Édouard were delicately interspersed with quotes from the deceased. The first page opened with words addressed to Brother Dominique on February 24, 1958: "A Father of the desert, at the moment of death, exulted with joy. When asked the cause, he replied: 'Because I have never done my own will.'" The images captured from above gave a great impression. The open coffin was placed on a large catafalque. It seemed to dominate the choir and the nave, which appeared tiny. Near the coffin, six large candelabras had been set up.

On that day, Dom Antoine Forgeot was subdeacon. He assisted Dom Jean Prou, the abbot of Solesmes. I could clearly distinguish the young monk in a photo where the celebrant was censing and blessing the body of the deceased. Dom Forgeot said to me: "It was very beautiful. There were four absolutions. Tradition, for a prelate, demanded it."

The burial took place in the afternoon. The community gathered with some family members. The album ended with three photos of the tomb, located in the apse. The stone was now sealed; the monks had engraved the simplest inscription in capital letters: EDUARDUS ABBAS † *1896–1962*.

When I met him again the next day, Dom Antoine had brought a large magnifying glass. He wanted to review the images of the funeral. Suddenly, he appeared like an old monk copyist, bent over his parchment. Scrutinizing the photos up close, he could recognize the abbots who had come to Fontgombault in large numbers — Saint-Wandrille, Quarr, Wisques, Kergonan, Ganagobie, Ligugé, Clervaux … the faces of the abbeys flashed by. The nobility, fatherhood, and warmth of Dom Roux remained intact in his heart. Dom Antoine took the time to look at the photographs of the deceased's face. For him, the moment was charming and moving. For me, it was extraordinary.

The largest album was dedicated to Dom Roy, the successor to Dom Roux. An intelligent, quick, and precise monk, he ushered in a new era for the abbey. More spiritual than mystical, more theologian than philosopher, he was a man of government and decision with a joyful character who had retained a childlike soul. He had been a hunter in his youth and continued to love nature and long communal walks.

A photo from July 2, 1962, showed how much the community had grown. Around Dom Roy there were fifty-four monks. In a picture taken during the summer of that year, he was discovered with his own family. It was an image of the happy France during the Gaullist years at Fontgombault.

A walk in the countryside with the brothers, shelling green beans; a general chapter at Solesmes in 1964; a trip to Rome during the Second Vatican Council; a visit to Mount Cassino and a trip to Ganagobie in 1965; the laying of the first stone for the new building for the lay brothers at Fontgombault; an audience with Paul VI in 1967; prayer before the Virgin of Dom Guéranger in Rome the same year; the search for an abbey in Auvergne, still in 1967; the Roman *Congresso* of Benedictine Abbots at *Sant'Anselmo all'Aventino* in 1968; days of rest in Castagniers, Provence, in the winter of 1968; a stay at the Hauterive Abbey in 1969; a visit to the Montserrat Abbey in 1970, in the extraordinary company of a hermit; and to the Valsainte Charterhouse with the great Cardinal Charles Journet in 1970; then with the choir novitiate of Fontgombault, of which Father Antoine Forgeot was the zelator. The images swirled, lively, moving.

On May 2, 1970, in the group photo of Fontgombault, there were seventy-nine monks. In less than half a century, the monastic troop had more than tripled its size. Soon, fifteen monks would depart for the Auvergne mountains to found the Randol Abbey.

Dom Jean Roy, builder, architect, wise man, left a solid legacy. Often, when speaking of him, Dom Forgeot would say "my father abbot." His death was tragic. In 1977, at the age of fifty-six, he died suddenly. He was in Rome for the *Congresso* of abbots. Father Jean-Louis de Robien, his secretary, and Father Doat accompanied him. One early morning, in the general house of the Cistercians, he collapsed in front of the door of his room, felled by a heart attack. A nurse tried to revive him, but his soul flew away a few minutes later.

The community was sad, stunned, and helpless. Dom Forgeot is convinced that he felt his last hour coming. In his personal affairs, which he had not had time to put in order, the monks found a prayer on death. He had just copied its stanzas. In 1976, he had wanted an architect to prepare his tomb. His private secretary had written a letter to carry out his request. He specified that there was no hurry. Rereading the letter, Dom Roy had written in the margin: "But what does he know about it?" One afternoon, in the cloister, he confided without preamble to Dom Forgeot that he didn't have much time left. He felt that his days were numbered. Yet, he had just undergone a cardiac examination and showed no worrying signs. Dom Forgeot has not forgotten: "He was magnificent, courageous, upright. We owe him what we are."

The first color album was dedicated to the abbatial blessing of Dom Forgeot. On December 8, 1977, on a cold day, the images showed the still-present pain and the joy of a promising election.

The abbot emeritus did not linger on the pictures of that day. Everything related to his person was of no importance. His humility was, once again, edifying.

To show support for the monks, the crowd had gathered for the blessing. Several bishops were present, and the priors of Grigliano and Randol assisted Dom Forgeot. In the final shots, one could see Dom Prou, who greeted the new abbot before returning to Solesmes.

Many monks whose faces we contemplated in the albums had died. What could Dom Forgeot feel when seeing these men whom he had known so well and who rested in the cemeteries of their monasteries? The former abbot revealed nothing, calm, unshakable. As always.

X
The Hermit's Caves in the Mist

Facing the abbey, on the other bank of the Creuse River, nature becomes almost wild. In the cliffs carved by the river, several caves are nestled against one another, like small, aligned houses.

In the early eleventh century, eremitism experienced a new resurgence in the Kingdom of France. Through edifying examples, these solitary individuals aimed to preach to their contemporaries the necessity of a return to the Gospel.

This corner of Berry offered a perfect setting for men in search of a hidden life. Chosen as a retreat by an anchorite named Gombaud, it soon became a thriving lavra (a monastery consisting of a collection of cells or caves) under the administration of Pierre de l'Étoile.

Eight caves remain. Passing Gombaud's rather spacious

"cell," next to a fountain famous for its water, the visitor enters a series of excavations, some of which are narrow and not easily accessible. The last cave, near a chapel rebuilt in the nineteenth century by the Trappists, is more extensive. It is supported in its center by a massive pillar carved into the rock. Given its size, it likely served as a communal room for the hermits. It is charmingly called "Chapter of the Hermits."

Near the shore, clearly visible from the abbey, the chapel, recently restored and dedicated to St. Julien du Mans, was originally a modest wooden oratory.

In 1091, due to an influx of vocations and the limited space, Pierre de l'Étoile decided to cross the river and establish a cenobitic monastery under the Rule of Saint Benedict. Thus, for a while, hermitages and the monastery coexisted.

The modest tomb of the monk named Gobert, who died in 1130, was found last century near the chapel. With his body, a plaque was discovered, inscribed as follows: "*Hic requiescit corpus gloriosissime indolis viri Goberti monachi sacerdotis. Hic ab infantia virgo Christum amavit. Obiit V idus Augusti*" ("Here rests the very glorious body of the good monk and priest Gobert. Here, a virgin since childhood, he loved Christ. He died on August 9.")

In the mid-twelfth century, the last hermits disappeared definitively.

However, in 1970, a Benedictine from Fontgombault wanted to rediscover this solitary life.

His name was Pierre Rotgé. Born August 17, 1930, he entered the monastery in 1950, took solemn vows in 1956, and was ordained a priest in 1963. In the late sixties, he asked the abbot to be allowed to go to the caves. Dom Roy was quite surprised, but he did not want to oppose the burning desire of his monk.

For a long time, he had secretly harbored a hermit vocation. During recreation, Dom Rotgé was always eager to be finished with it. On Easter Monday 1970, he crossed the river and settled in the excavation just above the chapel.

Father Rotgé was originally from the nearby village of Lurais. From a family of poor laborers, he lost his mother when he was age five and his father at nine. Taken in by an uncle, he had to quit school at the age of ten and later completed his studies. He worked hard from farm to farm. War soon broke out, and he didn't eat well. One day, he knocked on the monastery door to get a vaccine. He came to take care of his body, but left aware that he needed to take care of his soul. A beautiful journey began.

On March 30, 1970, on a cold and misty morning, he settled into his new cell. It was without comfort, electricity, or running water, a cave of about ten square meters. Nothing more. This extraordinary and disturbing life was full of mystery to me.

During my stay with the prior at the abbey in August 2019, we first went to greet him at the infirmary, then crossed the Creuse to visit the places of his hermitage. I looked at the beaten earth floor, the low entrance of the excavation, and the simple passage in the stone where the hermit had once placed his bed, not far from a small makeshift stove. Although the place offered a beautiful view of the abbey and the surrounding forests, I found it difficult to imagine that a man could live here, in such a harsh and austere environment. It seemed almost inhumane to me.

Father Rotgé had brought nothing with him. He had a small wooden table, a chair, and a chest. He ate little, contenting himself with rice, vegetables, cheeses, or fruits that kind souls left in front of the cave. One day, villagers left chocolate with a note: "For the not-crazy hermit." When recounting the anecdote to his brothers, much later, he added, "Not crazy, not crazy … " with a questioning look. Deprived of comfort, far from people, a short distance from his brothers, he was happy. Every Saturday evening, during vespers, so as to avoid meeting anyone, he came to the abbey to fetch meager provisions.

Ascetic, determined, courageous to the point of complete self-forgetfulness, he earned the admiration of the monks. The hermit returned to the abbey on rare occasions, taking the opportunity to quickly consult some newspapers. He wanted to be present for the tonsures, which always took place in the scriptorium, as well as during Holy Week, Easter Sunday, and a few major festivals. An eyewitness and olfactory-aware monk vividly remembered the Candlemas day when Father Rotgé burned his beard in the choir with a processional candle.

As a novice, Father Rotgé did not have extensive knowledge. He wanted to catch up. During a long stay in a sanatorium, the young patient spent all his free time delving into studies of painting, drawing, bookbinding, French grammar, Latin, English, German. Since then, he tirelessly sought to improve his knowledge, especially on a wide range of theological subjects. In the hermitage, using old dictionaries, he learned Greek, Syriac, ancient Hebrew, and literary Arabic. After a few years, he had an encyclopedic knowledge of the Desert Fathers: Isaac of the Cells, Moses the Ethiopian, John of Thebes, and Macarius of Alexandria were his friends. Father Rotgé took great care of their books, placing them in plastic boxes to protect them from moisture. In the summer, there was no danger: The caves were cheerful, surrounded by game-filled and verdant woods. In winter, the adventure became more challenging: The icy wind and thick fog covered the entire shore with a sinister shroud, and the sun's rays rarely managed to pierce the cold.

How can one endure long years in such spartan conditions? How can one not get sick? Monks who witnessed this epic affirmed that Father Rotgé prayed continuously. Prayer was the only flame that truly warmed his heart. Sometimes, from the abbey gardens, the lay brothers saw a shadow weaving through the trees. They knew that the brother recited the Rosary while walking. In the cave, it was impossible to stand up: The ceiling was too low.

In 1981, Father Rotgé had to leave his strange paradise. His spine was dislocated. He joined a new hermitage in Provence, under milder skies.

Upon his return to Berry, he confided to the monks that the most challenging part was by no means the solitude. No, the most challenging part was when God did not speak.

In the last months of his life, in the small infirmary cell, a prisoner of a body worn out by asceticism, he continued to pray every hour of the day. According to the infirmarian, he was the most delightful patient he had ever known. Father Rotgé's face was illuminated by the pure smile of children. On his sickbed, he maintained intact humor.

One morning, his doctor came to take a blood sample. So, in the evening, the infirmarian taking care of him tried to brandish the supposed results to get him to eat: "Do you know what the doctor said after your analysis?" He responded without hesitation, "That I shouldn't worry too much."

The prior remembers a particular visit. Sitting in a large medical armchair, the old monk said to him with a smile, "Ah, you come to delight me with your face." And one afternoon, seeing Father Abbot approaching, he exclaimed with his little high-pitched voice, "Here comes the good shepherd!" Every evening, Dom Jean also came to give him the blessing of compline.

And then, a brother asked Father Rotgé, "What will you say to the Lord when you meet him?" The answer was quick: "Oh, how poorly I loved you!"

"And to our dear Saint Benedict?" Father Rotgé exclaimed, "the best possible things!" Saints always have an astonishing propensity to find a thousand faults.

In March 2019, he was at death's door. Despite his respiratory distress, he continued to recite the Rosary with tenacity. His fingers continued across the small black pearls. In a state of semiconsciousness, he clung to prayer like a little child learning to swim clings to his float.

The Grim Reaper announced itself at the dawn of the following year. Dom Pateau had to leave for a week for the Ligugé Abbey. On the day of his departure, he came to visit father in his room. The ninety-year-old old monk had a fever, he was weak. But he understood that Father Abbot was asking him not to die in his absence.

Three days before his death, a brother was feeding him yogurt. Father Rotgé wanted to thank him, as usual. He said softly, "yes," then "thank you." And he never spoke again.

The dying man remained conscious until the end. However, on the last two days he no longer responded to his brothers' solicitations. On Sunday, after none, Dom Antoine Forgeot recited for him the last prayer for the dying. The community gathered in the room and the corridor.

Upon his return, on Monday, January 13, Father Abbot went to see him. He spoke to him and placed his pectoral cross between his hands. Father Rotgé became a little agitated; the time was around 12:30 p.m. During dinner, at about 7:45 p.m., a brother warned the abbot. Death was approaching. Dom Jean left the refectory to hurry to the infirmary: He hoped that he would still be alive. But Father Rotgé had just breathed his last breath. His face was peaceful and serene; he smiled. Father Abbot gave him conditional absolution.

Brother Rotgé died alone. Like a hermit.

It had been a long time since the monks had seen him. The infirmarian monk missed compline to wash him. Around 9.30 p.m., the prior was the first to begin the vigil, then the older monks took turns. All night, hour after hour, until the funeral.

Dom Jean scheduled the ceremony for Wednesday, January 15, 2020. That day, it was cold and beautiful. The monks were aware that they were going to bury Gombaud and Gobert's little brother, the last link in the millennial chain of the Berry hermits. These men were leaving forever.

XI
Visit of a Future Pope

It is Saturday, July 22, 2001. The Fontgombault Abbey is preparing to host a meeting of international importance dedicated to liturgy. Bishops, abbots, priests, religious, theologians, scholars, and carefully selected laypeople are converging on the lands of Berry.

In the evening, around 8:15 p.m., Cardinal Joseph Ratzinger arrives. The monks have gathered in an orderly manner in front of the grand porch of the abbey church. The prelate's car descends the grand alley, and all eyes are on him. The bells ring vigorously. Dom Antoine Forgeot kisses the cardinal's ring as a sign of respect and devotion. The prefect of the Congregation for the Doctrine of the Faith appears as himself — dignified, simple, and fraternal. The community is moved.

To the sound of the choir organ, Pope John Paul II's collaborator enters the great nave; the building always makes a strong impression when entered for the first time, and the wonderment is seen on his face. Then, he walks down the central aisle to kneel before the altar of the holy Sacrament. After a collation served in Father Abbot's parlor, Cardinal Ratzinger joins the beautiful episcopal cell. The next day, Sunday, he celebrates the Conventual Mass at the high altar.

The cardinal graciously agrees to talk with the community in the chapter room. Joseph Ratzinger speaks at length about his work in the congregation, his exchanges with theologians, and particularly his efforts to denounce the pernicious effects of the dictatorship of relativism.

After lunch in the refectory, he joins the conference room located in the extensive library of the guesthouse. His masterful introduction focuses on the intrinsic link between the crisis of faith, the crisis of the Church, and the crisis of the liturgy. Specifically, he posits that Catholicism has lost the true notion of sacrifice. Following one of his mentors, the theologian Romano Guardini, Ratzinger developed this thesis in one of his greatest books, published a few months earlier, *The Spirit of the Liturgy*.* Contributions from various participants follow. The cardinal is attentive.

Then, on the evening of Monday, July 24, he is invited to provide a conclusion. Out of humility, he first declares himself incompetent:

> I dare not propose conclusions; I did not have the time or the intellectual and physical ability to prepare something. I can only offer a few remarks. But above all, I want to express a very deep thank you to you, dear Father Abbot, for the spirit of this monastery that has inspired us with the peace of the Church, the peace of Our Lord, and thus allows us to seek together this Catholic

* Cardinal Joseph Ratzinger, *The Spirit of the Liturgy* (Paris: Ad Solem, 2001).

> ecumenism in which there can be reconciliation within the Church, in its differences that are profound and painful.[†]

Not surprisingly, the cardinal's impromptu conclusion is brilliant. He speaks for an hour. He notably mentions the importance of a "reform of the reform" of the liturgy:

> Professor Spaemann is right: the "reform of the reform" naturally refers to the reformed missal and not to the previous missal. What can be done, given that ultimately our common goal — it seems to me — is liturgical reconciliation and not uniformity? I am not for uniformity; but, of course, we must be against chaos, against the liturgical fragmentation, and in this sense, also for unity in the observance of the Missal of Paul VI. This seems to me a priority issue: how to return to a common reformed rite — if you will — but not fragmented or left to the arbitrary control of local communities, or a few groups of commissions and experts? So, the "reform of the reform" is a question that concerns the Missal of Paul VI, always with the aim of reconciliation within the Church because, for the moment, there is rather a painful opposition, and we are still far from reconciliation, even if the days we have lived here together are an important step toward this reconciliation.

He adds, clear and determined:

> It is important to me to maintain the possibility of celebrating according to the old missal as a sign of the

---

† Cardinal Joseph Ratzinger, "Assessment and Perspectives: Concluding Conference at the Liturgical Days of Fontgombault from July 22nd to 24th, 2001," *News from Christendom*, October 8, 2009.

> Church's permanent identity. For me, this is the main reason: What was until '69 the liturgy of the Church, the most sacred thing for all of us, cannot become after '69 — with incredible positivism — the most unacceptable thing. If we want to be credible, even with this slogan of modernity, it is necessary to recognize that what was fundamental before '69, remains so after: It is the same sacredness, the same liturgy.*

These words spoken at Fontgombault would later become a supporting pillar of his upcoming pontificate.

At the end of the conference, the cardinal goes down to the guests' courtyard. Everyone can talk to him. Father Abbot Antoine recalls a man "of great affability, perfect gentleness, extraordinary delicacy."

To the monks' great regret, the high prelate leaves Fontgombault on Tuesday morning around 7:30 a.m. Before his departure, Dom Forgeot invites him to enter the abbey church at the exceptional moment of low Masses. The cardinal is seized, almost speechless. He remains in meditation for a long time, kneeling on the floor at the back of the building. As he leaves he says, in a low voice to Father Abbot, who still recalls the precise inflection of his voice, "This is the Catholic Church!"

"These days are very beautiful memories," the former abbot confided to me in a whisper. How can one forget, in turn, the intonation of Dom Forgeot's voice when he uttered that simple sentence?

In the secret of prayer, the friendly bond between the cardinal and the abbey has always remained alive.

---

* Ibid.

XII
Dying in the Shadow of Notre-Dame

In the shade of cypress and parasol pine trees, under the charming gaze of a luxuriant wisteria running along a small wall, the deceased monks of Fontgombault rest in peace. The setting of their final sleep is enchanting.

In the summer, under the scorching sun, the scent of nearby orchards reaches the enclosure of the dead. In every season, for hours on end, the notes of the organist rehearsing pieces from the sacred repertoire cross the walls of the abbey church. The departed travel in music.

I have come to this place often. In the center, the stone cross, perched on its small promontory, overlooking the two tombstones of the Trappist abbots, has always reminded me of a lighthouse. That morning, with Dom Prior, we talked about the lives of the deceased. On the thirty small white stone crosses, the dates, the names of the monks engraved in Latin, lined up:

R.P. Xaverius Forgeot, Nov. 26, 1956
R.P. Philippus Vilain, May 24, 1956
R.P.D. Gilbertus Isambert, June 23, 1960
R.P.D. Georgius Dutfoy de Benque, Sept. 11, 1995
R.P.D. Robertus de Lamarzelle, Dec. 7, 1992
R.P.D. Theodoricus de Finance, Apr. 11, 1961
Fr. Clemens Pitard, Jun. 20, 2012
R.P.D. Yvo Chauveau, Jul. 2, 2015
R.P.D. Joannes-Michael Barais, Aug. 11, 2015
Fr. Paulus Papilleau, Oct. 12, 1968
R.P.D. Franciscus de la Blanchardière, Jan. 23, 1969
R.P.D. Albanus Saguez de Breuvery, Aug. 2, 2018
R.P.D. Andreas Bourdon, Nov. 18, 1973
Fr. Antonius Bouvet, May 28, 2015
Fr. Josephus Maria Jannot, Nov. 20, 1976.

The first monks of the twelfth century were undoubtedly buried around the apse. Then the cemetery was arranged in the enclosure where it still stands. Near the north transept, Benedictines and Trappists who succeeded each other since the thirteenth century are buried in this plot of land. Their mortal remains await the day of resurrection.

Today, when a monk passes away and his brothers dig his grave, their shovels often catch the stone sarcophagi of the Trappists, and sometimes skulls or bones. They distinguish between the Benedictines, buried perpendicular to the nave, and the Trappists, whose bodies are parallel to the building, with small metal nameplates placed on the shreds of their habits.

This calm place was highly conducive to remembering the touching conversations I had with Dom Antoine Forgeot. We talked about the death of his blood and religious brother. At the time of the latter's death, Dom Forgeot was at his bedside, accompanied by Father Abbot Édouard Roux:

> He died in peace. I was twenty-three, and my brother, twenty-five. We were prepared. At that time, there was no possible healing. For monks, death is dreadful, like a punishment; but it does not frighten us. It is natural. Hope gives everything. We are sure that death will not separate those who have loved each other on this earth.

Dom Forgeot had spoken to me with discretion about this painful tragedy in his life. A few months prior to his brother's death he had lost his father, aged forty-nine. And in the same year, 1956, he also saw the young Brother Philippe Vilain die. Both men had professed on the same day. Brother Xavier and Brother Philippe departed within six months of each other. The young shoots of Fontgombault departed like summer wheat falling on stormy evenings.

As death approaches, the monks' problems ease and simplify. Complicated, impetuous, or individualistic monks find serenity. Dom Forgeot always believed in paying attention to these signs, for they herald the end: "It is beautiful to see a monk aging well. God is faithful, and he helps us only if we let him."

The monks always try to accompany their brothers with great delicacy. For Dom Jean Pateau,

> the care of the deceased bodies is not so much about the fleshly envelope as the memory of the person. The respect for the monastic corpse shows that it is not a simple mass of cells. A soul has escaped; its flesh and bones are entitled to the attention of those who have lived with the deceased. We keep almost nothing that belonged to

> the deceased: a rosary, a crucifix at most. We burn notes or archives. After death, the body has the same scarcity. But it is not about making up the dead to give them a younger or happier appearance. This practice turns into a carnival, and it turns the deceased into a disguised mannequin. This theater tries to reassure the living. The monk who has left, lying on his bed, is the focal spot. He reminds us of a brother we love. The corpse invites us to meet the soul.

Often, Dom Forgeot prays at the grave of his elder brother. When the need arises, he takes care of the wisteria. He comes to trim the long stems of the woody plant that runs on the cemetery wall. In the shadow of the immense facade of the north transept, the final resting place of the brothers is peaceful. But for the monks, the issue really doesn't matter. They are oriented toward eternity.

On the Day of the Dead, November 2, the monks come to place two or three bouquets of chrysanthemums on the graves of their departed brothers. Throughout the year, the gardeners take care of about a hundred pots that will honor the deceased. They traditionally place a white chrysanthemum in front of each grave. Then they scatter flowers of all colors — yellow, orange, burgundy, mauve, fuchsia pink — trying to remember the taste of the deceased. I counted no less than eighteen pots around the large cross. The monks also like to adorn the two tombstones of the Trappist abbots whose memory is somewhat forgotten.

The cemetery has become a small, colorful, and vibrant domestic garden. When I visited, time seemed to have stopped. But the winter rigor would soon put away these sweet impressions.

XIII
Dom Prior

It often happens that the appointment of the prior brings about serious scandals in monasteries. This occurs when some, inflated with a wicked spirit of pride and imagining themselves to be second abbots, arrogate tyrannical power, maintain scandals, and cause dissension in the community. This happens especially in places where the prior is appointed by the same bishop or the same abbots who instituted the abbot.

It's easy to see how absurd this is, since right from the start of his establishment he's given something to be proud of, suggesting that he's been removed from the power of his abbot. You, too, he will say to himself, have been established by the very ones who instituted the abbot.

From this arise jealousies, conflicts, detractions, ri-

> valries, dissent, disorders: because when the abbot and the prior are thus divided in sentiment, it is impossible for their souls not to be in danger of such discord. Likewise, those under their guidance, taking sides for one or the other, go to their ruin. The primary responsibility for this danger lies with those who have become the authors of such disturbance.

In that exerpt from the *Rule*, Saint Benedict's words about the prior are not very favorable. Church historians often agree that the founder of the order must have encountered disagreements with his own priors.

Fortunately, on the banks of the Creuse, this is not the case. It is difficult to imagine Dom Pateau saying of Father Jean-Baptiste that he would have swelled "with a wicked spirit of pride." It's also hard to imagine the archbishop of Bourges compromising to impose a monk of his choice.

From a distance, the prior of Fontgombault looked like a young man — a hurried, serious, focused teenager. On this feast of Corpus Christi, he was overseeing the preparations for the ceremony. I had the impression of observing a passionate scout leader, a bit authoritarian.

But the image was deceptive. The monk whom the abbot chose to be by his side in the government of the abbey is a man who seeks wisdom and, even more, a courageous monk, filled with great energy.

His voice is deep, calm, and words wrap around. He utters a sentence, retracts, corrects to add another. He has one idea, then a second, but the two contradict each other a bit. There is concern. The exercise seems uncertain. Where are we going? Suddenly, he picks up on his statement and things become brilliant.

Dom Prior is precise and confused, pugnacious and timid, sensitive and determined. Three character traits, in particular, stand out: gentleness, intelligence, charity. Men who have had the grace to retain a childlike spirit often show this temperament, which makes them wonderful beings.

Certainly, it takes courage to follow the abbot of Fontgombault. The tutelary shadow of his predecessor, Dom Chauveau, is intimidating. But Father Jean-Baptiste is not afraid.

He was born November 22, 1983, the youngest of a family of six children. After his baccalaureate in economics, he joined the military Prytanée of La Flèche to prepare for Saint-Cyr. A young recruit, he entered the monastery in 2003, less than twenty years old.

My interlocutor always showed great politeness, a disarming delicacy. We talked a lot about monastic life. I teased him by asking if monasteries were not submarines and monks the inmates of a celestial prison. I know perfectly well that Benedictines are not prisoners. The real prison is sin, wounds, dramas of the past. Man comes to the monastery for God. The monk wants to free himself from everything that prevents him from being united with him. Dom Prior's response delighted me: "Monastic life is not a bed of roses. Thorns are many. Let's not forget Saint Augustine who said: '*Ubi amatur non laboratur et si laboretur, labor amatur*' ('Where one loves, there is no hardship, and if there is hardship, hardship is loved.')."

Father Jean-Baptiste dedicated his thesis in moral theology to the virtue of mercy. In these pages, he reflected on the notion of freedom. The monk made a free choice. Each decision involves difficulties. Don't let go at the first storm. Perseverance is crucial.

Father Jean-Baptiste was appointed prior at thirty-one. How can one become the abbot's principal advisor at such a young age? Doesn't giving such responsibilities to a young monk rob him of his religious life prematurely? In this case, the story is complex since the former holder of the office died suddenly. So, everything happened very quickly from the beginning. He was ordained a priest in 2012 by Archbishop Armand Maillard, and then, on February 2, 2013, he became the zelator of the choir novitiate. Finally, in October of that same year, he was appointed choirmaster.

Dom Delatte liked to say that the prior is the man of the abbot. The trust between the two must be perfect. This is confirmed at Fontgombault. The two men do not necessarily have the same points of view, but they agree on the basics.

In an abbey, the counselor's function has its rightful place. Dom Pateau listens with interest to the opinions of Father Jean-Baptiste. One advises, the other decides, and the proximity is strong.

Father Jean-Baptiste also takes care of the maintenance of the woods, which include forest parcels and parks. I concluded that he needed to expend himself physically, and, indeed, he told me he liked this work. This was not the case for his predecessor, who was pure soul.

Above all, I was eager to ask my interlocutor a simple question: how does one remain a good young monk? He answered immediately that it was important never to idealize monks: "It's not about magnifying our lives. The risk is great. It's one thing to make long speeches about obedience and humility. It's another to put them into practice and to pray. There is the ideal and the reality. Our authenticity is silent."

Dom Prior's youth was not without difficulties. It's hard to imagine a long, quiet river. More experienced monks can always show some annoyance. But the community did not pose any problems.

Sometimes, young monks become more cautious than the elderly. The prior of Fontgombault is of this caliber. A monk who knows how to alternate gravity and smiles, rigor and flexibility, was therefore the right person in the right place.

"The challenge of monastic life is to live freely within a strong framework constituted by the *Rule*, customs, and practices," Father Jean-Baptiste explained to me. And:

> At Fontgombault, history is everywhere. The places are anchored, reassuring, maternal. We must live with God. That is the only criterion. Does the contemplative want to persevere in his search? One does not become a monk by sheer will. Voluntarism makes no sense. The good monk does not give himself for the pleasure of giving himself. He gives himself to God. The nuance is important. The abbots help us. Their fatherhood transcends all eras. We believe that one must give oneself, but, in fact, one must learn to receive from God through the community. We must hide in him. We must consent to move forward.

Father Jean-Baptiste was not always certain that his vocation was at Fontgombault. He came to the Berry abbey for the first time at the age of seven. It was Palm Sunday. He kept three specific memories of that visit. The child had been impressed by the procession. Then, in the refectory, sitting at the end of the table, he had dropped his knife, bent down to pick it up, smiling at Father Abbot: "I understood well that the monks came to kneel before Dom Antoine when they dropped something." In the distance, at the novice table, Brother Pateau, who looked like a high school student, probably saw nothing of the scene. And in the afternoon, from his four-foot-height, he had asked Father Henry out of the blue, "Are you happy?" The good Benedictine burst into laughter.

The young man never thought of the vocation before his first year of high school: "I felt called to the contemplative life by Eucharistic adoration. I remember a very specific moment when the call was clear and sharp." He regularly returned to Fontgombault with the scouts or with friends. He hesitated between two communities, but the desire for an exclusively contemplative vocation prevailed.

How can one endure? The danger of activism always looms; a monk can play a role, get lost in trivialities, illusions. Dom Roux used a very apt metaphor. He compared the monastery to a bag of pebbles. The monks are stones in this bag; they clash and polish each other. This is how characters are refined, provided they play the game.

A monastery is a family, with its faults and qualities. What place does Father Jean-Baptiste have in this community? The prior is the elder. By his shyness, his simplicity, his idealism, one might imagine him in the place of the youngest in a large family.

A good monk is alone before God. But he lives in a brotherhood. An abbey is an incandescent microcosm, hidden from the world, but whose rays attract. This attraction is paradoxical. In fact, the monk is the one who takes the means to go to complete his baptism. Monastic life is a total Christian life. In a monastery, everything is connected. The farmer, like the baker, the florist, or even the abbot, must always give the best of their time to God, to the detriment of their obedience if necessary. Everything is free. A monastery can progress in each of its members and conventually. The three vows, obedience, conversion of morals, and stability, take shape in a family.

In his novel *L'Oblat*, Joris-Karl Huysmans wrote beautifully: "A true monk has only one homeland, his monastery."* It could be added that monks are detached. The further they advance, the less they see clearly. They have only one homeland because they are hidden in God. This is the memory that Dom Prior leaves with me. A hidden Benedictine, a Fontgombault Benedictine.

Others may see Father Jean-Baptiste differently than I have known him. This is the prerogative of a man with a big heart. He gives a lot. Everyone receives in their own way.

---

* Joris-Karl Huysmans, *L'Oblat* (Paris: P.-V. Stock, 1903).

XIV
The Wisdom of Father Master of the Choir Monks

A young man aspiring to become a monk would like to be sure that God wants him to give his life to him. His desire is understandable. Why enter monastic life? Monks often utter these mysterious words: "We have received a call."

In a monastery, it falls to the master of novices to help aspirants discern the authenticity of their choice. But no one can understand the secret of their vocation. The novice master is not the one who must separate the wheat from the chaff, the good students from the slackers. Vocation is not an excellence award.

The simple question that must be asked is, Does the candidate truly seek God? The novice master delicately places small pebbles on this path to help the candidate find his way. Does he show zeal for the divine office? Is obedience a burden for him?

Will the thousand little inconveniences of Benedictine life be overcome? These are the clues that Saint Benedict gives in his Rule. The novice master is a mountain guide who ropes in the candidates to lead them. But he does not know the way. To reach God, only the Lord knows the path. The role of the novice master is to show the candidate how to see the Light, how to listen to the Word, how to avoid crevasses, how to climb. But he must accept that it is God who truly leads him where he wants. Each vocation is personal. Each path is unique. The master of novices can support the candidate in discerning the right path. This already requires a lot of humility, self-resignation, to accept the will of God. But he can do nothing more.

The abbot entrusts this role to seasoned monks. At Fontgombault, there are two novice masters. One oversees the choir monks, the other the lay brothers.

For seven years, Father Jean Troupeau, who entered the abbey in 1979, has taken on an exhilarating and difficult task alongside young men who want to become choir monks. Previously, he was also a farmer and then a porter. His knowledge is not infallible, but he has great experience. He is a ferryman, a wise man who steers the monastic boat for those who are leaving one world to join another. Delicacy, empathy, rigor: The list of qualities he must demonstrate is long. If he lacks them, failure is assured.

During our meeting, I was struck by his calmness. The man is not very tall. He smiles little, expresses himself through brief phrases in a soft and human voice.

Was my interlocutor a doctor of the soul? I had the odd impression that Father Jean, when talking to me about the young monks he watched over, was diagnosing and prescribing. Perhaps he was even about to indicate the way to the pharmacy. Yet I was not addressing the infirmarian!

On the morning of our meeting, my interlocutor explained

things to me simply: "God has a plan, or he doesn't."

To illustrate his point, he spoke to me about two young men who had come to the abbey at the age of fifteen. "I asked them to think, reassuring the parents," he said. "They completed their baccalaureate. Over the years, one seemed quite lukewarm, hesitant, the other was very sure of himself. In the end, the first has just entered the monastery, while the second no longer wishes to become a monk."

With his usual gravity, Father Jean considered that the advances, hesitations, and swerves of young people who come to the monastery are not worrisome. Their lives are tumultuous; they do not easily reveal themselves. It is necessary to classify, throw away a lot, selectively sort through the heart to reach the spiritual goal. Time and patience are the real weapons.

God is free, undoubtedly. However, the vocational paths were simpler in the past:

> Family wounds, emotional gaps, and the brutality of experiences are difficult walls to climb. I think of a boy who always sat at the back of the church. During the services, he cried. Despite his fragilities, he wanted to enter the abbey. But he could not overcome some anxieties. Perseverance is important.

Vocations are joyful, painful, luminous mysteries. The interplay of grace and free will intertwines. The novice master is present to make each aspirant understand that his freedom is primary: "It is he who will say yes or no. God asks a question. Everyone can answer as they wish, sometimes even refusing to hear." God proposes, man disposes, and according to the *Rule*, it is with the grace of God that he can acquiesce

A monk who has not made this long journey is unlikely to endure. The novice master must listen to the voice of God and that of the aspirant. And when the sounds are lost in the night, the profound desire to give oneself to God is the only compass.

Each vocation is unique. In the nineteenth century, Saint Thérèse liked to say that souls are more different than faces. The kaleidoscope remains just as varied today.

The novice master recalled a boy who entered the monastery after a successful professional career. The rectitude of his approach was impressive. He wanted to build a first life in the world to be sure he had not cowardly fled it. He did not want his monastic choice to be made by default. When he had achieved his secular life goals at the age of thirty, he gave up everything to take the road to the abbey. Now, he is a happy Benedictine.

In 2020, candidates are older than before: It is rare for a man to enter the monastery before the age of twenty-five. Since 2013, the master of novices has received sixteen young men. Nine of them chose other paths and left the banks of the Creuse. A priest who dreamed of monastic life realized that the asceticism of the sons of Saint Benedict was not for him. A member of another congregation did not linger either. The mountain was too steep. The daily life of the past, the unique rhythm of contemplatives who obey a rule, and nostalgia for the world, are dreadful thorns.

Self-dispossession is the keystone of the monastic path. The monk is a man of obedience. He is no longer the master of clocks. His days are entirely organized according to a time whose use he does not decide. "In the West, the only value that remains is freedom," noted Father Jean Troupeau. "In an abbey, we choose to give God that very freedom."

In Berry, the novitiate lasts for five years. During our interview, there were seven wanting to become monks. The father master knows that the young shoots are vigorous if he sees a balance being struck between joy and rigor: "A man who devotes himself to God will always make sacrifices. But the pain is assumed, offered, and transfigured. God's peace gradually settles in the novice's heart. Time does its work."

Monks are aware that novices must often learn to live with old wounds. Flourishing is not a mechanical thing. Monasteries have nothing to do with places seeking well-being. A contemplative seeks exclusively the peace that comes from God: The life of sacrifice radiates throughout the Church. Does the novice master realize how difficult this phrase is to understand for the contemporary world?

Monks are aware that their way of life can never be adopted by the masses. Only a tiny elite of God can follow the rule: "God sends candidates, but we will remain a small family. In the Middle Ages, the blessed time of monastic radiance, the monks accomplished considerable works, but they were already a minority."

Father Jean is very lucky. He regularly sees young people who manage to transfigure the difficulties of their lives to become men of God. They do not deny them. They consent to look at them, eye to eye, to find joy. The monk does not seek happiness for himself. He desires God.

"Heaven gives in abundance if you seek it," Father Jean told me again. In a monastery, the link between asceticism and joy is the key that opens many doors.

How can one define external asceticism? Common life, a rustic existence that refuses the comfort that the world could give it, poverty, and regular manual labor are the framework of Benedictine days. Idleness is an unknown word. Like entertainment.

Common life is not a bucolic walk, but rather a way to thrive. It reveals narrowed hearts. The community helps each one to purify himself. A monk who seeks to isolate himself from others or to rebuild personal autonomy is in spiritual danger. Selfishness is a clever beast: There is no need to imagine that its tentacles stop at the doors of monasteries. The group is a protective net that cannot be a place of penance: "The community must expand the heart."

Moreover, obediences cannot constitute diversions from spiritual life, or this adulterated joy would become a deceptive romanticism for glossy-paper advertising.

During the novitiate, the elders teach customs to the younger: how to put away your napkin in the refectory, how to walk in the corridor, how to place your book in the choir, how to address Father Abbot ... Obedience is everywhere. These little disciplines may seem very picky to the world. For the monk, they are never optional.

The novice is an apprentice. He walks slowly in the footsteps of those who preceded him: "You do not push the doors of a monastery to reform the rules. You enter to receive fifteen centuries of tradition. Unity is the leaven of common joy." The monk sacrifices so that unity is preserved and joy reinforced.

The newcomers diligently read the *Commentary on the Rule of St. Benedict* by Dom Delatte, a veritable Magna Carta of monastic life at Fontgombault. Dom Guéranger's successor published this lengthy text in 1913, in which he wrote:

> We exalt ourselves in disobedience; it seems to us that we demonstrate energy and personal vigor: but Saint Benedict declares that it is simply cowardice and laziness; and if he qualifies the opposite attitude as work, he will soon tell us about its real fruitfulness and incomparable nobility.*

Rustic life should not pose an obstacle to true and deep vocations. However, at Fontgombault, the damp coldness of the church is an integral part of asceticism. In the vast abbey, except for the censer and the bellows of smoke rising, the monks, in the

* Dom Paul Delatte, *Commentary on the Rule of St. Benedict* (Paris: Plon-Nourrit et Cie, 1913).

heart of winter, have no other source of warmth. If a young man cannot withstand the monastery's cold, then what happens?

"It could be a sign that he is not meant for Fontgombault," Father Jean replied. "Each must adhere to the common observance. The severe cold is characteristic of the abbey for several months. The number of hours of sleep also factors into these considerations."

A young man from Latin America once entered the monastery. After a few months, he suffered terrible headaches. He went to rest with his family and felt better. However, upon his return, the pains reappeared. Father Abbot had to accept the idea that God wanted something else for him. Today, he is a bishop. The moral of the story: There is what man wants and the abilities that God gives him.

Monastic life can be trying. The intense rhythm and unyielding monotony of daily life can stir buried wounds. Yet, in an abbey, there's no escape; no distractions to create illusory bandages. Monks are men who face Pascal's challenge daily: "All the unhappiness of men comes from one single thing, which is not knowing how to remain at rest in a room."†

Novices who must leave the monastery are inevitably marked by their failure. The bonds, the laughter, the tears remain etched in their memory. Sometimes it takes years to turn the page. For the monks, the feelings are different. They don't forget those who left, especially those who stayed a long time. But the community moves forward without looking back.

Father Jean often talks about the "purification of vocations": "The search for oneself is the great pitfall. We must consent to destroy our old ambitions so that God can establish his love." There is no one-size-fits-all in monastic life. Each monk has a unique story. Growing pains are necessary. The contemplative who doesn't experience suffering, the mystic enclosed in celestial

† Blaise Pascal, "Divertissement," in *Pensées*.

joy, are myths: "God allows tears for growth."

Obedience reveals this inner asceticism: "A monk truly obeys when his thoughts align with those of the superior. In contingent matters, one must know how to renounce one's judgment to follow that of the representative of Christ in the abbey." Obedience extends to the intimate.

Saint Benedict aims for peace of the heart and defeat of the spirit of murmuring. However, a monk can always turn to another superior if an order should trouble him to the extent that he feels unable to fulfill it. He must refuse to carry out what is morally unacceptable because, ultimately, for Saint Benedict, it is always Christ whom one must obey. This understanding is not sought by all congregations. It would be inconceivable for the Dominicans, the Franciscans, or the Carthusians.

In Saint Benedict's view, spiritual infancy comes at a cost: The monk becomes a dependent child again. It is therefore a daunting responsibility to be an abbot: "We all want to walk in the same direction, toward God."

Dom Pateau is the lead climber. Beware of the fall.

Thus monastic joy lies in docility: "An inner light from God shows the insignificance of human things. Only God can fill the heart." These were the last words of Father Jean Troupeau during our meeting. The monk understands everything and nothing. He cannot answer a young man who asks, "Father, please tell me that I have a vocation."

God leaves us free.

XV
Walking with Lay Brothers

"I am at the service of Father Abbot, but I must not take his place." The statement allowed no contradiction. The monk who spoke to me seemed to hide his shyness behind the thick lenses of his glasses.

Dom Arnaud de Saint-Chamas is the master of the brothers. He is the vicar of the abbot to the brothers and lay novices. These outdated, hieratic titles conceal an eminent function.

Moreover, this great, reserved monk is also an artist. Pottery, goldsmithing, and time in a workshop occupy a significant part of his time. From his skilled hands come many crosses, vases, or magnificent chalices.

He sometimes speaks like a teacher possessed by the burning desire to advance his students. His demonstrations are precise. That day in June, I was hardly surprised to hear him tell me that he felt great joy in taking care of a school of prayer — an unusual term for Benedictines who are primarily contemplatives — attended by children from the surrounding area.

I remembered this monk well. Often, in the refectory, I had seen him take care of Father Alban de Breuvery, the former cellarer. Father Arnaud was seated next to the tired old monk. He would bring small spoons of mashed potatoes or custard to his mouth. He knew how to care for a sick man who was completing his earthly journey. His patience was extraordinary.

Father Arnaud is responsible for the spiritual, intellectual, and practical training of the brothers. At Fontgombault, there are eighteen lay brothers and three novices among the sixty monks in the abbey.

The day we met Father Arnaud immediately wanted to explain to me what made the monk under his charge special:

> The lay brothers have a beautiful vocation. It meets the expectations of young people who want a life more largely dedicated to manual labor. As monks, the lay brothers primarily want to give their existence to God. Then, their specific vocation is a life of service in material obediences that require a more sustained presence. There are also educated men who join the brothers out of humility. In no case should they be seen as the abbey's servants. They are religious in their own right. They do not all have the same formation and program of reading. This is also the case with the choir fathers, but the latter must complete the course of ecclesiastical studies.

Nowadays, many monasteries have abolished the special status of lay brothers. Often, this vocation has remained misunderstood. At Fontgombault, there are two novitiates, one for the fathers, the other for the brothers. A canonical barrier — that is, a separation between the novices and the rest of the community

— exists to preserve the novices in training. At the end of the novitiate, the monks should only speak to one another for work and charity purposes, or to render a service.

Throughout their lives, fathers and brothers will have relatively separate everyday lives. The buildings where their cells are located are separate. All the monks meet only at the beginning of recreation, before going their separate ways. On the other hand, on the day of the great walk on Thursday and on feast days, they stay together.

I have met many monks. I knew that their sense of community life allowed them to create a great unity in which all know each other well.

How did Father de Saint-Chamas define his obedience?

> The charge is magnificent because I take care of souls. I am the amazed witness of daily progress. Difficulties often come from community life. A monk is not in a monastery to do what he wants but to respond to God's will. The monk should not do what he likes, but like what he does. The contemplative does not enter a monastery to exercise an office, but to be a monk.

As I pondered these remarkable words, a question came to me. How does the brother remain joyful when a charge he loves is taken from him?

> The least gratifying obediences — housekeeping, laundry — are often the richest spiritually. Repetitive work is meritorious; it corresponds to the Benedictine vocation. We teach the novice that he does not enter the abbey to perform enriching work. The contemplative is not in cloister to have a beautiful life. We are sheltered from the worries and joys of the world. But the monk does not

> seek to find a more peaceful life. He must not settle into the comfort of routine. He cannot forget the reasons for his monastic vocation. We have come to a monastery to respond to God's plan. Loving God does not mean taking advantage of God. The monk should expect no reward.

How, then, does the monk manage to accommodate this repetitive life? He must overcome small annoyances by looking higher:

> I can tell myself that at the end of the world a man is converting because I offer my suffering for him. One does not overcome difficulty by resting, but by giving it meaning. God makes suffering fruitful. We follow the example of Christ. And it is the role of the father master to be present to help climb the slope when it becomes too steep.

The monks rely on one another. Fraternal charity, an expression that seems outdated to many, is a pillar of Benedictine life. When a monk sees a brother struggling, he comes to his aid. This charity allows them to bear the weight of the hours.

Prayer, study, and reading times allow for a more serene approach to challenges. However, if the machine is tired, the monk is vulnerable to all sorts of falls. On dark days, everyday life becomes heavy. The life of prayer in the choir and the life of work loses their depth. A monk may not realize he is living as if asleep. A sad monk loses his soul. He has no inner energy: "He is unwell; he has not given enough. He wanted to keep for himself a treasure that he could share. A monk must give everything. Spiritual nights are never overcome alone. Father Abbot is there in these deserts."

Everything is about surrender. In writing his charter on the day of his solemn profession, the monk tries to write as small as possible at the top of the parchment. The blank space under the lines symbolizes the void that God will fill. In monastic life, God can write whatever he wants, it is he who leads the monk as he pleases.

The Benedictines' long leather belt recalls Christ's request to Saint Peter: "When you were young, you fastened your own belt and walked where you would; but when you are old, you will stretch out your hands, and another will fasten your belt for you and carry you do not wish to go" (Jn 21:18). By this symbol, the monks tell God, "Lead me where you want me to go."

Make no mistake: The monk offers his freedom because he knows that God will never put him in jeopardy. In taking the vow of obedience, he has no doubt of the spiritual benefits he can expect. His monastic interest simply lies in not doing what he wants, but what God expects.

Individualism, materialism, and the insatiable desire for movement are the enemies of the contemplative man. They can prevent young people from taking the step of entering the monastery. It also happens that those who knock on the doors of the abbey have already taken on routine habits of old bachelors. But the monk does not have time to sit and dream. His schedule is precise. The Benedictines are sure that God still calls as much; only, many men do not realize it.

"I can understand the young," Arnaud confided to me. "When I received God's call, I was afraid. I ran away. I went the opposite direction." After high school, he wanted to enter Saint-Cyr. As a student, he had everything planned. His application had been accepted for preparatory class. During the Easter holidays, at a retreat in Fontgombault, the novice master asked him why he wanted to join the military school. He replied that he wanted to defend beautiful values. The monk retorted without flinching, with disarming simplicity, "A monk does the same thing." Then, he mysteriously felt that God was calling him, without understanding what was happening to him.

He cut his stay short. Leaving the guesthouse, he thought he would never come back. He did not want to become a monk. He refused to understand his spiritual thirst. At that time, Arnaud de Saint-Chamas was a scout leader. With his baccalaureate in hand, his troop was supposed to go on a horseback camp in Norway. At the last moment, the adventure stumbled upon logistical problems. The leader proposed replacing this exceptional trip with a camp … at Fontgombault. Arnaud was quite annoyed; he understood that God was insisting.

This winter, a young man said to him, while smiling, "You know, Father, we should not think too much about the generosity of the heart, otherwise we risk catching the vocation." Casual phrases sometimes scream with truth!

Let us not deduce that the young man who becomes a monk has a more generous heart than others:

> Returning to Fontgombault, I knelt before a cross. I asked God, "If I say yes, what will happen?" I quickly understood that I had to enter. I had little doubt about the sacrifices to come. I would no longer ride horses. I would not skydive. I would not enter the military school. I would not become an officer. But I would be faithful to God's plan for me

Father Arnaud said "yes":

> God always gives more than we expect. In a monastery, we do not see God, but we know he wants our happiness. A child instinctively knows if he is doing good by looking at his parents. Monks are always children. They cannot quantify the good of their prayers, but they

> know they are useful for the world.

A useful man is a happy man. A monk who knows the usefulness of his prayer is happy in the same way. It is not a frivolous joy. It is deep and stable. It is invisible. It has an unsuspected strength.

Before parting, I asked Father Arnaud if he wished to add anything. He did not need to think:

> Small acts of charity among brothers can illuminate a day and show that God exists. There are many different paths among the lay brothers. From converts to intellectuals who choose not to be choir monks out of humility, the journeys are diverse. In a monastery, the skills of the lay brothers accumulate with the generations. We benefit from the experience of those who preceded us. Sometimes, in the novitiate, the brothers have to overcome the frustration that comes from external views that underestimate them. They are generous, gentle, humble. They are fully monks, and they offer what God has placed in their hearts.

"One climbs a mountain and stumbles over a stone,"* wrote Georges Bernanos. The monks have made a wager. It concerns love. That is why they climb mountains, and many ravines too. The thing may seem heroic or crazy. Extraordinary or strange. The monks never ask themselves these kinds of questions.

---

* Georges Bernanos, *Dialogues of the Carmelites* (Paris: Seuil, 1995).

XVI
Like a Generous Cousin

Within an abbey, the monk known as the guestmaster is the first face encountered by those seeking the peace of the religious life. In the *Rule of Saint Benedict*, it is written:

> All guests who arrive shall be received as Christ, for he will say one day, "I was a stranger and you welcomed me" (Mt 25:35). Honor shall be shown to all, especially to those of the faith and to pilgrims (Gal 6:10).
>
> As soon as a guest is announced, the superior and the brothers shall hasten to meet him with all marks of charity. After praying together, they will exchange a sign of peace. This sign of peace shall be given only after the prayer, to thwart the tricks of the devil. …
>
> In this greeting, deep humility shall be shown to all guests, and whether upon their arrival or departure,

> Christ himself, who is being received, shall be adored in them by a bow of the head or a prostration of the body.

These words of the order's founder give the guestmaster an overwhelming responsibility.

At Fontgombault, Father Philippe took on this role on February 1, 2013. He was thirty-seven years old and had entered the cloister seventeen years earlier, on July 28, 1996. Discreet, even-tempered, and exceptionally thoughtful, he has no equal when it comes to teaching retreatants the customs and practices of abbey life.

The guesthouse is ideally situated near the monastic buildings. Along a long corridor, seventeen rooms, whose decor has not changed since the 1950s, welcome men of all ages who wish to pray with the monks. An oratory and a large library filled with numerous spiritual works complete this elegant and simple setting where each seeks God with their history, joys, and wounds.

Discussing his journey with the guestmaster, I understood the strength of the man before me. "Early vocations are increasingly rare. It's fundamentally a question of determination," he confided. His own case was a striking example: Against the advice of his parents and family, after five years spent in military school, high school, and preparatory classes, Father Philippe chose to become a monk.

The wise student loved sailing. He was naturally interested in the Naval Academy. "But the Naval Academy's exam coincided with the École Polytechnique exam," he said. "Rather than clinging to the Naval Academy, I took the accessible exams: X and Air. Rejected at the Polytechnique, I took the oral exam at École de l'Air and was admitted. I wanted to prove to myself that I was not a failure." This brother had insisted on completing his exams, but he had already heard the call a year earlier: "With a friend, I came to the abbey, officially to study. I wanted to see the master of novices. I asked for a meeting. My first impressions of Fontgombault are still very vivid in my mind. It was cold. The guest floor was deserted."

After that stay, the young man was certain of his vocation in Berry. Yet, as a student in La Flèche, he had hitchhiked several times with friends to the Abbey of Solesmes. He knew its great founder, Dom Guéranger, and one of his successors, Dom Delatte. He loved the beauty of the Solesmes pomp and Gregorian chant. But he preferred to join Fontgombault.

How can one be sure not to commit an error? "There are graces of blindness," he said. "God always hides many things from those he calls. If God showed us everything he will ask of us in monastic life, no one would enter. One must let oneself be carried away like a child who trusts."

Entering the cloister is the most important moment in a monk's life, a form of psychological shift: "The entire previous life is finished; the novice begins a life whose riches will never be completely exhausted." For a layperson, the rite of entering the cloister is disconcerting. In the morning, after breakfast, a young brother traditionally called "the guardian angel" comes to fetch the novice from his guesthouse room. The first few days are a second birth. The new recruit must learn everything of the smallest details: his place in the refectory, his stall in the choir, how to behave in processions, respect for customs in communal rooms, and a thousand other conventions.

A question haunts the novices. It keeps coming back: Will I be happy? Father Philippe was no exception: "When you come from preparatory classes, the novitiate can be a shock. In the first year, the priority is no longer the formation of the intellect, but the deepening of spiritual life. Monastic asceticism is the only pursuit." Father Philippe told me he remembered having the strange sensation of having switched off his brain. But self-detachment is the path to a new happiness.

After his priestly ordination, he returned to the path of studies with the preparation of a canonical license and now teaches fundamental moral theology.

In the novitiate, material tasks are constantly changing so that the young monk does not have time to become attached to any one thing. Similarly, today, his role as guestmaster is at the disposal of the abbot. Father Philippe knows his obedience means things could change overnight. He maintains a great detachment: "God watches over us." Until recently, Father Philippe was guestmaster and chamberlain, in charge of all the furniture, shoes, and clothing of the monastery. Father Abbot lightened his responsibilities, leaving him only the guesthouse.

Those who choose to come to Fontgombault often arrive happy at the prospect of their stay. Others carry heavy burdens of suffering. Their joys or sorrows are also those of the guestmaster, who must ensure that the retreatants genuinely seek God. The thirst for silence, among the youths as well as other age groups, is not feigned. On the contrary, it often proves to be unquenchable. The desire to flee noise, movement, and social trends has grown stronger over the years. Fortunately, shielded within the thick walls of the abbey, cell-phone reception is poor. Some even choose to give their devices to the guestmaster for the duration of their stay.

As early as May, young people come from across France to study for their exams. The countryside is green, the winter cold becomes a distant memory. In the perfect calm of the library, they are studious and focused.

Retreatants often like to share secrets with Father Philippe. The guestmaster entrusts many difficult situations to God, and he keeps those who come to him in prayer for a long time.

In the evening, when I was a guest at the abbey, I watched them walk in the park that surrounds the beautiful sixteenth-century building. A few hours after their arrival, the looks and smiles had transformed. Each found a small piece of peace. I thought of Christ's words: "Let the children come to me, do not hinder them; for to such belongs the kingdom of God" (Mk 10:14).

The work of welcoming, on behalf of his brothers, the men who come knocking on the monastery's door is magnificent. But the function is exhausting. It still happens that guests spontaneously present themselves at the abbey gate to find shelter and food: It is then the duty of the brother guestmaster to welcome them.

The stay of a retreatant lasts on average a short week. The guestmaster must not forget that he is not welcoming the retreatants for himself, but rather in the name of Christ. He laughed heartily while telling me, "If I got attached to the guests, I would be unhappy all year round." Dom Paul Delatte writes that an abbey has "four sacrificed ones": the abbot, the cellarer, the infirmarian, and the guestmaster. They have difficult tasks so that the monks can better live their vocation.

In 2004, Father Philippe was appointed choir zelator. In an abbey, this strange term refers to the assistant to the novice master. He loved this time in service to the young. Then he was the steward, responsible for the kitchen under the cellarer, and zelator of the brothers, in other words, the assistant to the novice master to guide the lay brothers, including the novices. This role allowed him to get to know this friendly group. Even then, daily life was not without its challenges. But joy remained.

The guestmaster at Fontgombault likes to consider that all monks must scrupulously remain in their respective places. "A happy monk is a faithful monk," he summarized.

Can a Benedictine monk, like the poet, cry when storms and tempests "weigh like a lid on the groaning mind prey to long sorrows"*? Father Philippe's words were gentle and wise: "If tears come, they are willed by God. He will always enable us to move

* Charles Baudelaire, "Spleen," in *Les Fleurs du mal* (Zurich: Librio, 2015).

forward." A monastic life without trials would be worrying. Conflicts abound. The happiness at the end of the road depends on how these crises are lived: "Perseverance is a great Christian and religious quality. We must remain daily with the Lord. Every day of our life. Let us be like little children, and all will be well."

Could the beautiful secret of the monks to happiness be so simple? The modern mind would be inclined to think that monotony is a great danger. In movement and noise, nothing is more dreaded than days that seem the same. The twenty-first century citizen consumer does not want to be a creature of habit. It's even their worst nightmare. The guestmaster often hears this question: How can you avoid not getting bored in a day that repeats itself identically, ten, a hundred, a thousand times? His answer, in the form of a question, remains unchanged: "Why change a stable and balanced way of life?"

For instance, it would never occur to a Fontgombault monk to question the time for matins. Waking up early is difficult, but the contemplative wants to reach God in prayer as soon as possible: "When we perceive the right place of each moment, we still have to enjoy it every day. Monotony is apparent. For the monk, each day is different. There are always discoveries. Nothing is ever banal."

A community knows its share of happiness and misfortune. For a monk, fraternal life is both the greatest penance and the greatest joy. In the world, if disagreements arise, one can always escape. Within the walls of the enclosure, the monk does not have this possibility. He must face problems. He is especially obliged to solve them. Otherwise, daily life is impossible. Each monk has an experience of the qualities or shortcomings of his brothers. Faults never completely fade away and can remain a source of suffering. Joy is found in the smallest things. The monk thus knows what he can ask of one or another member of the community. In an abbey, there is also a form of character adjustment worthy of a Swiss watch!

We often talked about the cold of the land of Fontgombault. Father Philippe concluded by saying that the choice of place has a decisive influence on the monk. Rooting in a geography is fundamental. A monk can be unhappy because they have not found the monastic home that suits them. The place assists in shaping souls.

In Fontgombault, in winter, the cold reigning in the church divides the postulants into two groups: those who question the temperature of the abbey church and the others. Father Philippe remembers that he never questioned the cold before entering the novitiate. In a way, he belonged to the category of "resistants." Today, it no longer freezes in the church, but Fontgombault's cold is damp and penetrating. It creeps into the bones unexpectedly: "The monks have gotten used to the cold," he assured me. "They don't even pay attention anymore."

In other words, the Benedictines no longer realize the rigor of the lifestyle they have accepted. The sheep's wool of their tunic is insufficient in winter, too warm in summer. And that's how it is. There is still spring and autumn. Monks often say that an office delayed by ten minutes can upset a monastic day. They are not wrong. But if the temperature in the abbey church were not to drop below five degrees (Celsius) in winter, it would result perhaps in a considerable change.

The monastic citizen enters a continuum where they are happy with God and their brothers. This corridor from which they never emerge is poetically called tradition. The ultimate difficulty of the novitiate lies in the suppression of singularities. Thus the choir novice must not put down his book even if he knows a hymn or an antiphon by heart. He must not stand out. They follow the example of the elders. Within a large community, the novice quickly understands that observance of unity is a factor of peace.

There is a fragile boundary between the establishment of community life and crushing personalities. The long Benedictine tradition has taught monks to respect individuals. Centuries of experience provide the keys to balance; wisdom doesn't come in a day. For Father Philippe: "When a monastic rule is too harsh or too lax, it is swept away by time. The *Rule of Saint Columban*, which had a considerable influence in France, was harsh. It did not survive." The *Rule of Saint Benedict* prevailed due to its gentleness and precision. Time tests the rules.

However, history can be a burden. The letter of the laws eventually kills the spirit. Commentaries on the *Rule* are precisely made to adapt monastic requirements to the spirit of the times. For instance, monks used to skip breakfast. Tradition dictated that the only meal be taken after sext. This practice was relaxed. In the last century, Dom Delatte, abbot of Solesmes, had a great influence.

Monastic history holds a thousand unsuspected riches. Before the offices of sext and none, one hears a hundred bell chimes, which gives the monks time to reach the abbey church. This tradition dates to the Carolingian era. The continuity is fascinating. The monk knows how to live. He knows how to die. He knows how to gaze. He knows how to smile. One could even say there's a rhythm inherent to monastic life. However, religious life is simple. A monk does not hide. He doesn't seek appearances. In fraternal life, masks fall off. Flaws and qualities quickly become evident. Each monk is the mirror of the other.

Guests feel happy spending a few days at Fontgombault. By observing the monks, they feel like they are putting their lives back in order. The experience is paradoxical because they can never live in the world like Benedictines. But the retreats are cleansing. People come out more rested.

The Benedictines welcome university professors, doctors, motorcyclists, scouts, high school students, penniless students, beggars, young fathers, retirees, happy or depressed men, believers, agnostics or atheists, priests, seminarians. In the refectory, the large guest table never looks the same. Anything is possible.

XVII
Beautiful Walks

It was thirty-six degrees in the shade and forty-two degrees in the blazing sun. On Thursday, August 6, 2020, in suffocating heat, the monks set out for their weekly walk.

Guests and families sought refuge beneath the lime trees, children slept under the trees in the grand alley, but the Benedictines didn't hesitate to bravely face the merciless rays beating down on the tortured countryside. Wearing large, prehistoric straw hats and old, patched clothes, they ventured into the shaded paths lining the Creuse River. Would the dark river offer a bit of respite? That was far from certain. Nevertheless, they set off cheerfully, as if embarking on a long journey to distant lands, smiles on their faces. Business as usual.

The oldest members stayed at the abbey, where the upper rooms, since the Middle Ages, hadn't lost their legendary coolness. Meanwhile, Dom Jean Pateau was absent, having gone to

Provence for the abbatial blessing of the abbot of Ganagobie.

The walk is a monastic activity just like any other. Admittedly, the *Rule* says nothing about these moments, but a monk cannot escape them. They strictly form part of the religious day, just like the Divine Office, meals in the refectory, or obedience. The daily recreation, after lunch, lasts forty-five minutes, differing from the Thursday walks, which last around three hours.

Recreation is a time for rest, a reprieve during grueling days where the notion of free time doesn't exist. Once the dishes are done, Father Abbot provides some news updates. In the cloister passage, he announces serious events, the deaths of illustrious figures, or more anecdotal items. Then the monks venture into the countryside. Usually, they head through the orchard, pass through the small north gate, and take the road running behind the monastery. During the weeks of lockdown, they never left the enclosure.

During their walk, the monks engage in casual conversation. The midday reading in the refectory often sparks endless debates. "Reading brings us together," confides one of them. There are also communal memories, deceased monks, and the minor events of obedience to discuss. Ultimately, they share everything and nothing. Recess isn't a place for first-rate theological jousting.

During these times, cultural differences between generations become evident. When Father Abbot announced the death of Johnny Hallyday (a French pop music star that many considered a national treasure), the older monks had no idea who he was talking about. Some explanation had to be given about the man whose funeral procession would descend the Champs-Élysées. From the national funerals of Victor Hugo — whom the monks knew very well — to the idol of the once young, there was a gap.

On Thursdays, the day of the weekly walk, vespers are moved up to 3:45 p.m. instead of 6:00 p.m. The monks leave the monastery around 4:15 and return three hours later.

Except for the novices, all monks, fathers, and brothers join the walk. They divide into groups between those doing the "average walk" and the "small" one. The older monks are often in the latter. The choir novices and the novice brothers form two separate groups. "When tired, it can be tough," a monk confided in me. "Some prefer the cold, others the heat. Hence, we can choose between the different routes. When we sit together, there are always jokers and storytellers who love to share funny stories. In summer, discussions in the shade of trees or in a meadow can last a long time."

In winter, the monks enjoy visiting the churches in the region to admire the Nativity scenes. Twice a year, each monk can take a walk of about fifteen kilometers with his family. Also, twice a year, in the days preceding Advent and Lent, there is a walk with a snack — typically pound cake or galettes with farm butter, accompanied by delicious monastery milk jam. Finally, once a year, the monks organize a full-day walk. They usually head to the banks of the Red Sea pond, one of the most beautiful in Brenne. On that day, the Benedictines leave at 8:00 a.m.,* say Mass outdoors, have a generous picnic lunch, and return tired in the evening for vespers, having walked about thirty kilometers.

The liturgical season has an impact on these moments. During Advent, there are recreations but no walks. During Lent, there are no walks and no recreation on Fridays.

How many delightful phrases about these recreational times have I heard? I cannot remember them all. I tried to jot down the funniest ones in a small notebook.

One day, a monk quipped with a smirk, "Monks' stories only amuse monks. In fact, they're children's stories." I found his remark quite true.

---

* The entire schedule is moved up: Matins is sung the previous evening, lauds and prime are in the morning at 4:50 a.m., to allow for the early low Masses to be said.

During a long walk to the Red Sea pond, it poured, and during lunch the monks' bowls filled with water quickly. A monk frowned: "Father Abbot had said the walk would happen if the weather allowed it. I wonder what weather doesn't allow it!"

Another time, a brother whispered to me, "Sometimes when the monk leading the walk is a bit intellectual, we miscalculate the distances and end up running so as not to miss dinner." He added this unexpectedly wise conclusion, "We don't go to recreation to relax, but to entertain others."

Another monk, in his prime, told me enthusiastically, "What I love most are the harvest recreations!" A bit surprised, I asked, "What do you mean, Father?" His response was swift, "Potato picking and grape harvesting, dear Nicolas!"

Recently, a dreaming monk learned that young boys no longer wore ties to school. His brothers were a bit stunned, but they refrained from mocking him. The walk is also a moment of community delicacy.

At Fontgombault, the Benedictines are fortunate to have a highly skilled musician, Father Jorge. He is, in a way, a recreation all on his own! Thrice a year, at Christmas, Easter, and the Assumption, he prepares a music recital. Recently, Bach's *Passion*, Handel's *Messiah*, and Mozart's concertos enchanted the monks. In the scriptorium, the organist presents and comments on the works. His abundant knowledge of music is never lacking. On another day, he selected *Magnificats* from different eras. The monks attentively listened to interpretations by Palestrina, Victoria, Charpentier, and Bach. The abbey also boasts a rich collection of sacred music or polyphony recordings. Following an ancient Solesmian tradition, from the first Sunday of Advent to February 2, on Sundays and Wednesdays, the monks gather to sing popular Christmas songs. Father Jorge sits at the synthesizer, and the monks sing the old hymns one after the other.

That's the fraternal life at Fontgombault.

XVIII
The Soldier Monks Stand Guard

Observing three monks within an abbey often conjures the image of soldier monks. The first handles the finances, the second the health of the bodies, and the last oversees the gatehouse and commerce. The term "soldier monk" was coined by Bernard of Clairvaux when speaking of the brothers of military and hospital orders: "It is as peculiar as it is astonishing to see how they know to be simultaneously gentler than lambs and more terrible than lions, to the point where one does not know whether to call them monks or soldiers," he wrote in *De laude novae militia,* "or rather, one cannot find other names that suit them better than these two since they know how to combine the gentleness of the one with the bravery of the other."*

* Bernard de Clairvaux, *Oeuvres complètes*, trans. Abbé Charpentier, vol. 2 (Paris: Louis Vivès, 1865).

The cellarer battles with numbers, the infirmarian fights illness, and the gatekeeper, at the bow of the ship, watches as visitors pass by, representing the world he has left behind. They are Benedictines of the battlefield.

Chapter thirty-one of the *Rule* states that "someone wise, mature in character, temperate, not greedy, arrogant, unruly, unjust, negligent, or prodigal, but filled with fear of God and like a father to the entire community shall be chosen as cellarer of the monastery."

Who is this virtuous man possessing such qualities? Does he even exist?

Saint Benedict continues:

> Let him take care of everything. Let him not do anything without the abbot's order. Let him observe precisely what is commanded. Let him not sadden the brothers. If a brother makes an unreasonable request, let him not cause pain by rejecting it with disdain; instead, let him reasonably and humbly refuse what is improperly asked of him.
>
> Let him guard his soul, always remembering the apostle's words: "He who has administered well thus acquires a high rank."
>
> Let him take special care of the sick, children, guests, and the poor, knowing without doubt that on Judgment Day, he will have to give an account of his conduct toward them all.
>
> Let him regard all the objects and possessions of the monastery as sacred vessels of the altar. Let him neglect nothing. Let him neither be stingy, wasteful, nor squander the monastery's patrimony, but let him do everything in moderation and in accordance to the abbot's orders.

> Above all, let him have humility, and if he cannot grant what is asked of him, let him at least answer with a kind word, as it is written: "A good word is still the best gift."
>
> Let him take care of everything entrusted to him by the abbot, and let him not involve himself in matters forbidden to him. Let him give the designated portion to the brothers without reluctance or resistance, lest they become scandalized — remembering the punishment divine Scripture threatens against those who scandalize the least of the least.
>
> If the community is large, he shall have assistants, so that with their help, he can fulfill his duties with a peaceful soul.
>
> What needs to be given or requested shall be given or requested at the proper times, so that no one in the house of God is troubled or grieved.

One remains astounded by this cascade of categorical demands. At Fontgombault, it's indisputable that the cellarer is a monk of experience. Father François has held his position for twenty-one years. But is he a man "wise, mature in character, temperate, neither greedy, nor arrogant, nor unruly, nor unjust, nor careless, nor profligate, but filled with fear of God and like a father to the entire community"? Only God knows.

The path of his youth seemed to lead him to different skies. From the Naval Academy, where Father François excelled, and throughout his years in the Navy, administrative and financial matters repelled him; he could never have been a naval commissioner. He was enamored with freedom. On the day of our meeting, under a scorching sun, in the shade of the large trees in the guests' garden, Dom François spoke like a child, proud to say to me: "Before going to Fontgombault, my great joy was burning all the papers in the big Breton fireplace at home, in the heart of the peninsula of Plougastel-Daoulas. I was sure I was done with paperwork." I couldn't help but burst into laughter. Decades later, this man found himself in charge of administrative and financial matters at the monastery.

A prosaic consideration constantly weighs on the life of an abbey: How to ensure that material issues do not stifle prayer? For one cannot pray when filling out an administrative form. Driving a tractor across fields allows for meditation, but tax returns are more obstinate. The farming brother enriches his meditation with birdsong and the movements of deer. The cellarer is more helpless when faced with registered mail and other notes from asset managers.

However, like all his brothers, he must foster peace and charity within the abbey walls. Dom Delatte wrote in his famous *Commentaire* that the cellarer must be "a strong monk."

Many abbeys have chosen to close their farms as bureaucratic hassles or profitability demands clouded the horizon. This reality left the cellarer of Fontgombault speechless. With his notary glasses hiding kind eyes, displaying his mischievous smile, he was sure that "at Fontgombault, by the grace of God, these difficulties have been overcome. The farm must remain a jewel of our manual activities. Here, one breathes in the beauty of creation, the taste of work and toil; one savors these products in our plates and those of our guests."

Moreover, the great asceticism of a monk is not being able to speak of God. The straitjacket of numbers and tables become the cellarer's prison: "In the world of administration, everything hardens and complicates. A soul is at great risk of withering if it's condemned to invest too much in it. When one spends life in accounting documents, one forgets how to open a book."

Father François is not bitter. He has kept a joyful soul. But his face occasionally reveals a severity attributed to arduous obedience. The cellarer sometimes dreams of the day when he will hand over the keys of his charge. A horizon emerges; in the distance, a hermitage … One understands that this idea crosses the wandering imagination of many monastic stewards. They dream of a cave in a mountain, a lighthouse on a deserted islet, of infinite spaces that would replace prefilled tax declarations and contribution slips. Cellarers need to imagine paradises without prefilled forms, pension contributions, or documents related to health standards.

One day, the abbot of Fontgombault had asked the abbot from Triors how to choose the best cellarer. The latter immediately responded, "Choose a theologian!" He meant to emphasize how deeply rooted in spiritual foundations the one taking on the role should be. A cellarer might spend seven hours of their day staring at Excel spreadsheets. The monk engaging in such draining work cannot embark on that venture without a solid monastic foundation.

Still, the cellarer wanted to reassure me: "My joy is the community. When I walk through the monastery and see all the monks happy in their roles, I am filled with peace. I understand that my efforts are not in vain. I am rewarded a hundredfold."

• • •

Now let's talk about the infirmarian. The holder of this office was Father Damien Thévenin for a long time. He entered the abbey in 1977, two days after defending his thesis, toward the end of his medical studies. Seven years later, he became responsible for the infirmary. After thirty-five years of service to the ailing monks, his tenure ended in September 2019. Replaced by Father Florian, he remains the medical doctor of the monks' community.

Father Thévenin still teaches Sacred Scripture and Patrology. "God seeks men. They are free to respond, to return home," he said. "The monk is the one who gives everything. Monastic life is nothing exceptional. It is simply a state of perfect life. The contemplative refuses to be scattered. He is focused on God."

The man in front of me spoke fast, his words colliding. Sometimes, a sentence escaped me. Nevertheless, he was confident in his reasoning. Listening to Father Thévenin, I felt as though I were attentively witnessing a lecture on a mysterious life in supraterrestrial catacombs. It's often the nature of family doctors: They have their feet on the ground and their heads in the clouds.

In an abbey, the abbot tends to the soul while the infirmarian looks after the bodies. The farmer tends to the cows, the gardener to the vegetables, the cellarer to the bank accounts, and the infirmarian to those injured by illness or old age. He keeps them, watches over them. And in the words of Saint Benedict, "he expects death."

The infirmarian carries his brothers. He cares for monks who haven't spared their bodies during lives often filled with exhausting work. At all hours of the day and night, the monks can knock on his door. When they become like children who can no longer walk, it is he who must help them bathe, dress, move, and eat.

For a long time, Father Thévenin was both a doctor and infirmarian. He prescribed the treatment and administered it. It was quite remarkable.

What does the *Rule of Saint Benedict* say about his role?

> Above all and before everything else, the sick must be cared for and served as if they were Christ in person; for he himself said: "I was sick and you visited me," and again: "What you have done to the least of these, you have done unto me."
>
> On their part, the sick should consider that they

> are being served for the honor of God and not vex their brethren who serve them with unnecessary demands. Nevertheless, they should be endured with patience, for thus a larger reward is obtained. Therefore, the abbot shall be particularly watchful that they suffer no neglect.
>
> A separate room shall be assigned to the sick brothers, with a God-fearing, diligent, and careful brother to serve them.
>
> Baths shall be offered to the sick whenever it is expedient; but to those who are well, especially the young, they shall be less frequently allowed.
>
> Meat shall even be allowed to the sick who are quite infirm, that they may recover their strength; but as soon as they are better, they shall return to their usual abstinence.
>
> The abbot shall be very careful that the cellarer and attendants do not neglect the sick, for he is responsible for all the faults of his disciples.

The infirmarian must know how to preserve his religious life. Especially since Father Thévenin has always been involved in the spiritual direction of the guests, he is a monk before being an infirmarian:

> One must not be a prisoner of an activity. The pitfall applies as much to the gardener, the cook, or the infirmarian. The monk must not allow himself to be absorbed by his duty to the point of forgetting that he works to reach heaven. The specificity of the infirmarian is often linked to the concern of making a wrong diagnosis. Thoughts can become obsessive. In this, obedience is unique.

Father Thévenin rarely shows his sadness when one of his brothers passes away. He sees death as liberation. I couldn't help but perceive in his somewhat cold demeanor a way of protecting himself. He had told me that "all monks must bear the burden of their brothers." A magnificent ideal. In that moment, just observing the charity in his gaze was enough to assure me that he made it his own every day.

He always looked calmly upon his work. "Pious, funny, fraternal monks can become taciturn patients," he said. "Others, solitary or reticent, transform into charming and caring residents. There's no rule. God decides."

Dom Thévenin sees monastic life as a school of charity. Behind the walls of the infirmarian, he doesn't feel superior to his brothers: "The infirmarian monk, the cobbler monk, or the farming monk must be filled with the same zeal. Charity is incumbent on all. Unlike the world, we do not seek perfection in our work. We seek charity and obedience until death. This doesn't mean that the infirmarian doesn't seek to heal his patients."

For a long time, Dom Thévenin didn't know the name of his successor. Then, in the fall of 2019, Father Florian took over the mantle of an infirmary that now houses three residents. In ten or fifteen years, if God grants him life and illness knocks on the door, the nursing monk will take care of him.

Father Florian is as silent as Father Damien was talkative, as secretive as his predecessor was a demonstrative man. The new holder of the office is a gentle, caring, and attentive monk. His program is simple:

> Treating the illness is important, but the man is not just his physical body. I want to listen, speak, understand the other. Above all, I must remain as humble as possible, not rush, and be patient. One can hurry to bandage or administer medication because they want to leave quickly for a rewarding activity. But the good infirma-

> rian is the one who doesn't count his time, and knows how to give it to his patients. Every day, I offered to the late Father Rotgé to escort him for half an hour or more to the infirmary's oratory, leaving him alone with his Lord. I also spent time talking with him in his cell. That time, I could have dedicated to nobler things. It was important, and I don't regret it.

• • •

Saint Benedict often found himself at the monastery gate, where he spent long hours reading. In chapter sixty-six of his *Rule*, titled "The Porters of the Monastery," he writes:

> At the door of the monastery, a wise old man should be placed who knows how to receive and deliver a reply, and is of a maturity that prevents him from running here and there.
>
> The porter should have his dwelling near the door, so that those who come may always find someone ready to answer them.
>
> As soon as someone knocks or a poor person cries out, he will respond *Deo gratias* or *Benedicite*, and with all the gentleness inspired by the fear of God, he will quickly answer with all the fervor of charity.
>
> If the porter needs help, a younger brother shall be assigned to assist him.

Centuries later, in his *Commentaire*, Dom Delatte also emphasized that the role of the porter has always been an important obedience.

Father Bernard is seventy-three years old. However, he is a young porter: He has been in this role since August 2018.

Every day, he welcomes visitors who arrive at Fontgombault. As soon as the fine weather returns, the porter's house near the abbey church attracts an influx of faithful, tourists, and the curious.

The monks sometimes share stories about this obedience. They recall, for instance, the late Father François de Feydeau. A brilliant student, he had gone through the Naval Academy, after which he disembarked from the *Jeanne d'Arc* to embark for good on the monastic life. His father didn't easily accept his vocation. When he learned of his appointment to the role of doorkeeper, he said in jest, "I guess they've showed him the door."

Father Bernard arrived at Fontgombault in 1973. Ten years after his entry, he was entrusted with the responsibility of the printing press. Dom Forgeot wanted to capitalize on his expertise acquired in student unionism. At that time, printing pamphlets held no secrets for him. Since 1999, he has also been involved with the Missionary Servants of the Poor in the Third World, a movement for which the abbey handles the French secretariat. In the porter's lodge, he now oversees the orders for articles of piety, books, and art objects that the monks offer to visitors. He is happy. "We bear witness without really noticing it," he said. "People are kind. They need to talk. They admire the life we lead and express their joy at having come to see us. Visitors marvel at everything, always wanting to know the number of monks. They sometimes express concern that we might not be very numerous. I reassure them."

Occasionally, tourists arrive at the small guardhouse ("Two tickets, please.") convinced that they need to pay to enter the monastery. Father Bernard must explain to them that the monastery isn't for visiting and that the abbey church is a place of prayer open to everyone, free of charge. Disappointment sets in: "But then, don't the historic buildings we see on postcards offer tours?" Armed with his patience, the porter explains it a second time.

In the shop near the porter's lodge, the monks showcase a documentary about life at Fontgombault. Tourists, initially seeking old stone structures, are reassured. If they visit the abbey during services, like vespers, they come out impressed. Because, like retreatants, they can join those services. Small liturgical sheets are provided to everyone at the church entrance. When they return to the porter's lodge to buy a devotional item, their faces are different. They appear calm, serene, at peace. The miracle of Fontgombault has worked.

More and more often, visitors come seeking protections. They buy medallions of the Virgin Mary, Saint Michael, or Saint Benedict — almost as a form of medicine. They seek a blessing like a holy grail. Despite this, the monks offer to bless devotional objects.

Father Bernard realizes that some are in search of a form of dubious magic. He must explain the meaning of genuine prayer and the path to finding God.

It's different for the monastery's faithful. They come to give a friendly greeting, acquire a book, or deliver a message to a monk in the community:

> We are here to listen. People need to talk. We must maintain great charity. The essence of the path lies in the attentive listening we offer. Sadly, we notice every day how much people lack someone to confide their sorrows in. They live in great solitude. Simply speaking is a beginning of a solution. In just a few moments, it's about finding the right words for those who share family problems, professional setbacks, or moral declines with us.

Monks do not bathe in the changing waters of the world. They left society on the day of their enclosure. The religious are broadly informed about the events of the country. One might think they are not equipped to understand the problems of an era they hardly know. Nothing could be further from the truth: They often manage to find the right words.

At Fontgombault, the porter's lodge is a warm little room. Certainly, the books might seem a bit cramped in this pocket-sized library. But it feels like the antechamber of the monastery. In addition to Father Bernard, present in the afternoons, seven other monks take turns.

In the evening, he goes over his accounts: "It's not exactly an exciting activity. I check sales and place orders." Nevertheless, he enjoys working with craftsmen who send him beautiful religious items.

In the *Rule*, Saint Benedict stipulates that the porter has a cell near the entrance of the monastery. If someone arrives at the door at night, Father Bernard must answer.

The beauty of Fontgombault attracts. People seek silence, and the monks are happy to be able to provide a few drops of spiritual happiness that is becoming scarce in the world. Upon closer examination, the greatest search is always for God.

The atmosphere in the porter's lodge is fraternal. Visitors often say beautiful things: "It's touching; we see that you care for one another." They are sensitive to the small gestures the monks make toward them. They feel as though they take away some of the monks' charity. Father Bernard is clear: "In the world, contacts are harsh. People no longer know how to look at one another. At the monastery, we take the time. People experience a kind of contentment when looked upon with kindness."

Paradoxically, visitors of a particular moment are interested in long-term matters. How do you live in community? How do you eat? How do you care for each other? How do you die? They perceive the simplicity of the monks' communal daily life.

They admire it. "In essence, you know how to live like men," one might hear them say. "In society, we've become robots. You have great respect for each other."

Ultimately, it's all of humanity that Father Bernard sees passing through. Agnostics, the curious, young retreatants who come to browse books at the porter's lodge, the faithful who request Masses for the deceased and know that the monks will be good intercessors.

All seek the products of monastic craftsmanship. The shop next to the porter's lodge is a must-visit. Shortbreads, eggs, meats, confectionery, and ceramics delight both young and old. Like a modern viaticum.

A porter's life isn't routine. Each visitor is different. The monks give them a lot. But the reverse is also true. Above all, visitors are observers. They scrutinize the monks' faces. They hang on to their words. They will remember even the smallest of phrases for a long time.

The daily life of today's porter isn't so different from that of the Middle Ages or antiquity: He leads a simple life. When relieved of their duties, porters return to a more traditional existence, away from the world. They were familiar faces; they depart into the shadows.

Fontgombault has an esteemed porter. Certainly, he is never called that. Yet, I couldn't help thinking of this title while meeting Father François. Perhaps it was due to the strong character of this former naval officer who entered Fontgombault in 1969.

He proudly told me that "Saint Benedict spoke of the monastery gate in the singular. In the past, the porter was the custodian of the only key to the abbey. This function has been replaced by the telephone. The porter is the one who receives calls for the whole house."

However, Father François is not upset about having left his

position. Now treasurer, he also manages the farm's shop. With his unaffected humor, he declared, "At the farm, I'm still a bit involved in business. I sell our good products and manage accounts!"

The treasurer doesn't handle finances but rather relics. At Fontgombault, in the side aisles of the abbey church, three imposing wooden cabinets contain the mortal remains of two thousand saints, bones, hair, or precious fabrics carefully preserved in beautiful reliquaries and the medallions of another time. Every day, he displays a saint's relic in the sanctuary. On the day of our meeting, Father François was searching for a relic of St. John the Baptist, which he placed on the main altar, highlighting the significance of the feast day.

What memory did he hold from his former life? The old father, who always seems to be emerging from an eternal nap, became more serious: "All social categories gather at the porter's lodge. That's its charm; alas, I've witnessed the degradation of people's religious culture. The breakdown in transmission is terrible. One must remain calm and patient. The grace of God helps in this."

He didn't want to write a testament for his successor: "There were too many things to say. I gave up on it. Father Bernard learned everything on his own. Anyway, he is much more organized than I am." Naturally, there is much admiration for Father Bernard.

The former porter has resumed his *lectio divina*. Before starting his work at the porter's lodge, he used to read the imposing *Expositions on the Psalms* by Saint Augustine. His duties prevented him from continuing. On the day after his departure, he opened the book to the page where he had stopped five years earlier. The book and its bookmark awaited him in his cell.

Within a monastery, love often passes through small things.

The porter's lodge is the realm of insignificant events. People don't always come there to find a bit of happiness. But they leave with a lovely share of the monks' felicity. As beautifully expressed by Georges Bernanos, "In every little thing, there is an angel."*

* Georges Bernanos, *Journal d'un curé de campagne*, *op. cit.*

XIX
Calves, Cows, Pigs

Near the stables and hay barns, next to the tractor garage, Brother Raphael-Marie's office was invaded by flies. June's dipterans are the most persistent of the year. They seem devoid of any sense of measure.

Brother Raphael-Marie is an exquisite man. He possesses the politeness of the old countryside, the kindness of men of the earth. He observes his interlocutor with a frank and simple gaze. With a complexion tanned under the low-angled sun, and skin weathered by the January chill, he advances with the measured step of the humble. Sometimes, his laughter seems slightly forced — often a mark of the shy.

The day I met him, under the stifling midday blue sky the thermometer already read thirty-four degrees. Inside the monk's room, it dropped to thirty. Our conversation kicked off in high gear. "The search for the infinite is always at the beginning of a vocation," he told me. With an Olympian calm, he continued: "I take care of the monastery farm. God is present in all things. He is with the calves, the cows, the little chickens, and the big pigs."

Born in 1967, when he entered the abbey at the age of twenty, he first worked in the vegetable garden, orchards, and in building maintenance. In 1990, returning from military service, he began his journey at the farm, starting with the evening milking of the dairy cows. For thirty years, it has been his kingdom.

As a child from Sarthe, he grew up in the countryside with no knowledge of agricultural life. However, he was already aware of the profession's difficulties. His opinion hasn't changed: "Farmers are exploiters in the best sense of the term, but they are exploited by the system. The reality is simple: the farmer works every day of the week, their salary is reduced to earnings, and they're always dirty."

The monk is fascinated by the eternal cycle that marks the seasons. He always seeks to make the best of things: "Nature disrupts plans made in advance. On Saturday, I wanted to make hay. The mower broke down. I searched for new belts. Then the rain came and interrupted my plans. And now, the heatwave has settled in. My schedule is topsy-turvy."

Fontgombault's farm spans seventy-five hectares, with mostly grassland, including twenty-five hectares of wheat, rye, spelt, and fava-bean crops. Corn cultivation has been abandoned. Lately, the brother has been trying to develop alfalfa. In 2010, the monks purchased a small combine harvester. Brother Raphael-Marie proudly mentioned it was a John Deere: "That's serious!" The mechanic monk takes care of its maintenance. They collaborate with other farmers; a neighbor bales the monks' straw, and the abbey threshes their grain. Additionally, the abbey has about twenty dairy cows and sixty Jersey cattle for fattening, providing the richest milk in fat and protein, from which the monks make excellent cheese. The grazing lands are clustered around the monastery, with acidic plots near the Creuse River. On the hillsides, there are rather dry clay-limestone fields that suit alfalfa well.

The farm, vegetable garden, and orchard are intended to provide the abbey with food autonomy. Profitability is not a priority: the brother refuses to plant soybeans that come from America or Brazil. Corn seeds, which require fertilizer, are no longer allowed at the abbey, which has reverted to an exclusive system. Simply put, the Benedictine farm's land has grown accustomed to not receiving fertilizer. Initially, yields decreased, but now they have increased. They had to wait for a new virtuous cycle to take hold. The brother explained that they use a lot of cow manure and work with some bacteria: "Alfalfa is able to fix nitrogen from the atmosphere. Why buy nitrogen manufactured with fossil fuels?"

The monastery farm aims to be an agricultural model respectful of nature: "In the fields, in the barns, I am always connected to divine creation. The little calf just born speaks to me of God. All our cows are *pro-life*." It almost sounds like a verse from a popular song.

Before me, the farmer did not hesitate to wonder if modern farmers have become the new slaves of consumer society:

> We know that a farmer's production can generate five or six salaries. The agricultural population represents 4 to 5 percent of the active population. The average weekly working hours are rarely less than sixty. The salary is never guaranteed. A storm, a period of drought, or excessive cold can wipe out a year's work. Similarly, if the global price of milk decreases, the local cooperative also reduces its payment. Farmers are rarely asked for their opinion. The system is terrible.

Brother Raphael-Marie said he noticed that the farmers he sees in photos in professional magazines often have sad smiles. He felt that those who had switched to organic production seemed more fulfilled. The earth is not a dumping ground where man can endlessly add fertilizers from shiny tractors.

The brother can recognize the type of livestock farm by observing the behavior of the animals. Some farms have cows that approach humans; they trust. At others, they flee. These latter animals have no real contact with the farmer: "At Fontgombault, we love our animals," he said. "I love seeing the animals and plants grow. There's nothing more beautiful than a naive little calf seeking its mother's tenderness. When a cow gives birth, she's exhausted. But she always takes the time to care for the calf before resting."

The abbey maintains excellent relations with the region's farmers. They consider Brother Raphael-Marie to be doing the same job as them. They sometimes see him in monastic garb, more often in his eternal beige work overalls. I was curious to know if he spoke to them about God. The monk told me that when a farmer asked him, he replied straightforwardly. "It's my cows that do the best apostolate," he explained. "They are calm and so affectionate that many wonder how I make them behave like that. During milking, they're serene. Kicks are rare."

Why do they have this attitude? The answer is simple:

> It all depends on the way we look at them. If we love them, they'll love us back. My cows know I respect them. I see all animals as a gift from God. It's not about becoming a pantheist! Behind nature, we must find him. A cow's lifespan is short. It doesn't exceed ten years. We must know how to enjoy the beautiful moments. A marvel appears by our side; we must look at it with joyful eyes. God gives it to us to better love him.

The cows even indicate the quality of his hay: "They separate the wheat from the chaff. If I present poor-quality grass, they'll let me know. In the feeding trough, I find the clunkers, but the good hay has disappeared."

The veterinarians who have long cared for the abbey's animals taught him the art of calving. The day he witnessed his first Cesarean section in the barn, he felt a little unwell:

> It's not nothing to see a cow's belly opened to let the calf through. It's a great struggle for life. The other day, I lost a little heifer who died from suffocation. She left in my arms, and I couldn't do anything. I tried to blow into her nostrils to clear the mucus, but the breathing didn't come back. You can't see an animal die without suffering.

Brother Raphael-Marie also takes care of the cheese-making. He produces butter, cottage cheese in summer, and Tomme cheese in winter. In summer, the twenty cows produce 250 liters of milk per day. "At the abbey, the fat content reaches seventy grams per thousand milligrams. At the supermarket, it never exceeds thirty-eight grams, and nineteen for semi-skimmed milk," he said, as proud as a rooster.

In the refectory, retreatants are often surprised by Brother Raphael-Marie's farmer milk's strong taste. The return to traditional values also passes through the bowl of milk in the morning!

The monk is horrified by synthetic milk and meat cultivated from stem cells. The abbey's farm offers its meat for direct sale. People are amazed by the quality and taste of the meat. For Brother Raphael-Marie, the meat is good because it has been loved. He criticizes cattle farming practices that don't allow animals time to grow. He doesn't care about yield: "The true farmer is one who takes care of his land. An operator inevitably seeks profitability.

But the care we give to our fields and animals cannot be reduced to techniques, accounting equations, and pesticides."

The monk marvels at everything. The summer moon, the long evenings of haymaking, the playful intrusion of a lizard into his office, the magnificent green of the wheat in the month of May: "God's gift is fleeting. We all pass. The only thing that remains is God's gesture."

On the day of our interview, he was concerned about the difficult start of the newly born calves (a slight diarrhea and some leave the world in a few hours). The monk is proud to see those he saved eagerly suckling their mothers. They drink and frolic contentedly. "But if a calf dies," he added, "God wants us to remain in praise of his creation. We are not in paradise. The earth is marked by original sin. Everything is a bit broken. We must follow Christ."

How could the monk live without his work on the farm? He admits that his daily life would be more difficult. But he also knows that life in nature is a source of suffering that he would no longer endure. When a cow he has known since birth leaves the farm, the monk is unhappy for several days: "In my life as a farmer, everything is tough and beautiful. When I was fifteen, I dreamed of a courageous, solitary and monastic life. God heard me, right?"

Of course, the monks come to help on the farm when needed. Brother Raphael-Marie is also closely connected with the lay brothers who take care of the orchard, the vegetable garden, and the father in charge of the vineyard and winery. In winter, he helps in the abbey's kitchen.

However, the farmer doesn't tend to the henhouse, over which Brother Charles-Marie reigns; the six pigs in the pigsty also depend on this pretty principality. A few days after my conversation with the farmer, I met this tall, smiling, and talkative monk who first came to Fontgombault at the age of three. His father, a history professor, loved conversing with the monks. Brother Charles-Marie shares with the farmer brother the conviction that if we are kind to animals — in this case, chickens — they become joyful and sociable. There are 230 laying hens. Additionally, he has installed broilers in the large orchard. A bit of a poet, our monk thinks that the monks are now in good company when reciting the Rosary. They eat the orchard worms: "It's good for the trees!" Brother Charles-Marie doesn't like the modern world. Recently, he had to travel by plane. The experience was unpleasant for him. He prefers the gentle poultry in his enclosure.

Listening to Brother Charles-Marie, like Brother Raphael-Marie, one would almost forget the demands of monastic life. However, the farmer is first and foremost a son of Saint Benedict. He recites his Rosary before attending the lay brothers' matins in the chapter room. Then, like the whole community, he goes to the abbey church for lauds and then serves a low Mass. After breakfast, he promptly heads to the farm and has the option of not attending the terce office, which he recites privately. Then he is in the choir for sext, none, vespers, and compline. In summer, Dom Jean authorizes him to skip services during the harvest. When the rain arrives and the wheat or rye is ripe, Brother Raphael-Marie hurries to the fields.

When the brother plants wheat or rye, he favors old varieties:

> With new cereals, constant weeding is necessary, otherwise the plants die quickly. Therefore, we cannot do without fertilizers. With organic techniques, the grains are better, and the straw is excellent for the animals. Chemistry damages the soil. There's much talk about glyphosate, but large amounts of nitrogen are also dangerous. How can one not admire the natural quality of the earth's microorganisms? The vicious circle of chem-

> istry is dramatic. We must reject this pattern and increase biological experiments.

Brother Raphael-Marie is convinced that local small farmers are the future of the profession. They are happy because they love their job and manage to make a living from it. He is outraged by suicides in the countryside. The suffering of these desperate families deeply troubles him. He knows the reasons. But he would also like to show the path to a new happiness in farming. He is a monk in love with God and nature. After our conversation, I was sure of one thing: The Fontgombault farm is a true ecological model that should be studied and imitated.

XX
Vegetable Gardens as Far as the Eye Can See

He entered the abbey a few days after the farmer brother. At twenty-five, Brother Jérôme-Marie had just completed his studies in English and literature. His family hailed from Lorraine and Burgundy. Dom Forgeot was unaware then that he had opened his doors to the two lay brothers who would feed the monks for years to come.

The brother humbly tends to the two hectares of the vegetable garden. Between the abbey and the first houses of the village, the rich market gardens of the monks make a strong impression. For a long time, Douglas firs shielded the monks from overly curious eyes; they have been replaced by a composite hedge of chestnuts, elms, maples, and elderberries: The Benedictines' vegetables need a certain privacy.

On a fresh November morning, as we walked between the rows of vegetables, the brother explained the secrets of his art. With a gentle yet determined voice, he began by saying, "The purpose of the vegetable garden is first and foremost the subsistence of the community and our guests." The brothers do not sell their vegetables. Yet, they cultivate no less than twenty-five acres of potatoes.

Winter vegetables were already emerging from the ground. Rows of leeks, beets, carrots, celeriac, kohlrabi, spinach, and lettuces were perfectly aligned in their little trenches. They had replaced the tomatoes, zucchinis, asparagus, melons, peas, onions, shallots, and green beans of summer.

The monks use green fertilizer methods and regularly rotate crops in the garden plots to allow the soil to regenerate. "I can transform a square of tomatoes into pasture, sow mustard flowers, or forage sorghum after growing lettuce," said Brother Jérôme-Marie. "The main thing is not to leave the land abandoned. I choose species that restore its richness. The potato enclosure, for example, changes every year." One can dream that these monastic rotations become the norm for all vegetable growers: People wouldn't have the same dishes on their plates anymore.

Near a wall, the monks pile small mountains of rotten vegetable and fruit waste. Kitchen vegetable waste that does not go to the chickens or pigs fuels the compost. The brother had also piled up a heap of dead branches and foliage nearby.

These organic fertilizers are spread on the soil in winter and spring:

> I cover the ground with branches and straw so that weeds don't grow. During winter, earthworms work below. They loosen the soil, bring elements down into the depths, then bring up trace elements. I plant or sow

> while maintaining this natural layer. The results are interesting. Nowadays, market gardeners too often work their soil mechanically, leaving it bare. Lands become poor and infertile faster than one might think. Nature is fragile. In the past, we used chemical herbicides that we have gradually banned in the abbey.

While we conversed, he was unaware of the poetry that could arise from his practical reflections. "We no longer grow lamb's lettuce," he explained. "The cultivation is too technical. But perhaps we will start again because the monks appreciate this small salad, which is especially crunchy at Christmas when the frost is strong."

The gardens are located on the edge of Creuse. They are damp, and despite the retention basins attempting to control the dark river, floods can cover all the land parcels. A little higher up, the monks have three large greenhouses, and a small one for seedlings. They measure thirty meters long by six wide. The hundreds of young spinach plants in their small pots will one day end up on the monks' plates, enjoyed in cooked salads. Brother Jérôme-Marie is the main provider of vitamins for the monks.

Further away, there are eggplants, peppers, and small tomatoes. Thanks to the heating resistors running in the sand of the frames, the vegetables never feel cold. Sainte-Thérèse greenhouse, Saint-Joseph greenhouse, Notre-Dame greenhouse, and the newest one, Sainte-Faustine greenhouse, each hold great importance in the abbey's gastronomic life. Finally, in the greenhouse dedicated to the adoptive father of Jesus, lettuce and chicory pleasantly coexist with cardoons and red cabbages.

Brother Jérôme-Marie is a valiant knight unaware of himself. He has declared war on pigeons, who have a guilty predilection for the garden's cabbages. With imperturbable seriousness, the monk meticulously covered the plantations with vast nets of fine mesh. He prepares his weapons against these "birds" with varied diets who leave nothing behind: "They spot the cabbages from afar. If I don't close the doors of the Saint-Joseph greenhouse, they can enter to devour everything. And when they come to peck at the cabbages, afterward, nothing else grows!" At the words of Brother Jérôme-Marie, whose speech suddenly accelerates, one measures the extent of the plague. This year, with tenacity and cunning, the monsters ended up eating everything. Fortunately, in the Notre-Dame greenhouse, the tomatoes and melons grow peacefully.

The monks harvest the first tomatoes in June. The production can last until All Saints' Day. At the end of the season, when the frost arrives, they gather the last green tomatoes that haven't had time to ripen to make jams: "You have to mix them with lemon pulp to give a good taste."

Two monks work permanently in the garden. Occasionally, another brother takes care of mechanical issues. "Fortunately," Brother Jérôme-Marie explained, "we have seasonal labor. For potato harvests, several monks lend a hand. In the afternoon, the guests, brothers studying theology, and novices can reinforce the small group." The monastic garden of Fontgombault is one of the largest and most diverse in France.

In recent years, unfortunately, there have been several shortages. During the heatwaves that struck the region, the harvests were almost nonexistent:

> The last three weeks of July, the zucchinis, which usually love the heat, gave nothing. Despite good watering, the flowers disappeared. In June, the first green beans had beautiful flowers, then the picking abruptly stopped. In spring, the lettuces were magnificent. With high temperatures, they became stunted. The monks couldn't eat them all summer. Melons, which usually love the heat,

> also couldn't resist. For the Solemnity of Saints Peter and Paul, our thermometer reached forty-two degrees. Gardens don't like such drastic fluctuations.

Not far away, the water from the dam seemed turbulent. It had been silent for several months. A light winter rain was falling on the countryside. The ground was damp, but Brother Jérôme-Marie wasn't wearing boots. He had simple open-toed black leather sandals. A few meters away, a young lay brother struggled to pull a large cart filled to the brim with cut fir branches. Ravens could be heard croaking on the banks of the river. Brother Jérôme-Marie rejoiced in this recent clearing: "For the garden, it was a catastrophe. They cast shadows, made the soil acidic, and their small needles flew into the vegetables. The brothers who prepared the salads in the vegetable cellar even had to be careful not to get pricked."

The gardener spoke proudly of a plot of land that the abbey had recently acquired. It had been left fallow for three decades. The monks cleared it meter by meter. It took two long years because brambles had grown up to six meters high. The monks crushed incredible quantities of weeds. Bordered on one side by a small drystone wall and by the Creuse river on the other, its soil would be rich and fertile.

Not far away, they had also planted a beautiful row of walnut trees, whose harvests would enhance cheese or pastries. The novices would gather them in October: "Walnuts are particularly appreciated during Lent. They are the little sweetness of fasting days."

In 2019, the monks harvested five metric tons of potatoes. Before the takeover of the Wisques monastery in northern France, where fourteen monks from Fontgombault went, the harvest even reached twelve tons!

Next year, on former potato plots, the brother plans to place young heifers with a foster cow. They will fertilize the soil. He has agreed with the farmer brother: "We won't place young bulls there. They would be capable of jumping into the vegetables and trampling everything." How rude!

Fortunately, there are guard dogs, two German shepherds, who love to forcefully show their presence. The kennels are close to the greenhouses.

The brother takes care of everything in his garden. Cloistered Benedictine monks need to live in simple and beautiful places. The vegetable gardens modestly try to meet this requirement, reaching for perfection.

XXI
Comice Pear, Gala Apple, or Reinette Clochard?

Brother Paul is a laundryman, cook, butcher, beekeeper, and fruit grower. Before entering the monastery, he was a schoolteacher. We are losing our Latin! Maybe he too, actually ...

He joined Fontgombault in 1983 and began working in the orchard in 1989. Upon arriving at the abbey, the young monk didn't even know how to prune fruit trees. He learned everything in the south of France where he briefly joined the new community of Gaussan, a foundation of Fontgombault. There, he was entrusted with the task of creating an entire orchard by himself.

In 1991, the winter in Berry was harsh. All the trees at the abbey froze. The monks decided to buy their fruits from an orchard in Limousin: "I realized that the trees were not pruned like they are at the monastery," he said. "That's when I understood the extent of the progress we needed to make. Those farmers from Haute-Vienne taught me everything, without asking for anything in return. But thirty years later, I still pray for them."

Behind the abbey church, Fontgombault's orchard is divided by a long alley that leads to a beautiful statue of Our Lady of Lourdes. On one side, near the north gate, there are trees bearing pips, including apple and pear trees. On the other side, in "La Folie," the name of the small house used as a honey room, there are stone fruit trees, such as plum, mirabelle, apricot, peach, and cherry.

Prune Valérie, Quetsche Stanley, Reine-Claude, Prune d'Oullins, Reine-Claude Dorée, Prune d'Ente, Golden, Fuji from Japan, Belchard resulting from a cross between Golden and Reinette Clochard, Gala, Sainte-Germaine, a Limousin variety, Pinova (Brother Paul's favorite — crisp and sweet), Melrose, Goldrush (a recent creation), Cybèle, as well as other types of apples; along with the following pears — Conference, Williams, Comice (originating from Angers in the nineteenth century), and Delbard.

On the morning of my visit to the orchard, novices toiled in the alleys, bravely weeding. Brother Paul wished to sow creeping clover to fix the nitrogen present in the air and restore it to the trees. Not to mention that bees love its flowers.

One year, the monks made seven hundred kilograms of mirabelle plum preserves: "We always keep preserves for two years. We are never safe from a season of severe frost that could affect the fruits.

The apple harvest begins at the end of August with Cybèle and lasts until the end of October. The community gathers fifteen tons. Brother Paul's accounting is more precise than an Auvergne apothecary's ledger: "A monk eats a hundred kilograms of apples every year, in compotes, pies, and as table fruits," he said. Approximation has no place in Fontgombault's orchard. A small portion of the production is sold at the monastery shop: "People are happy to taste our fruits. We offer good prices."

Brother Paul plants lavender near each row of trees to repel aphids. These pretty mauve bouquets smell like his former Occitan abbey.

Memories are abundant. The lay brother hasn't forgotten that he planted cherry trees in 1985 with Father Damien Thévenin. He also spoke to me about the vineyard. Along the trellises that run along the fence walls, there are table grapes. In 2019, the monks harvested three hundred kilograms. They start picking them at the beginning of September for the refectory's use. The first grapes are blessed during the conventual Mass. Some trellises are dedicated to making wine for Mass. In the nineteenth century, the Trappists had already planted pinot noir grapes. Brother Paul recalled the old, gnarled vines of a grape variety that didn't yield much anymore.

Each row of trees has an ingenious drip irrigation system for watering. In 2016, the abbey acquired an anti-freeze system. When Brother Paul knows that the temperature is dangerously low, he gets up in the middle of the night to open valves of large pipes that sprinkle cold water onto the tree flowers: "The water freezes the flower at zero degrees so that it is not damaged, and the temperature cannot drop any further." In a region where freezing is common, these advanced techniques have already helped the monks save two harvests.

From the heights of the orchard, the view of the abbey church is magnificent. We continued our tour. Here, Brother Paul mentioned that he intends to replant rhubarb plants: "In the past, we harvested four hundred kilograms a year. We could make exceptional pies."

Around a row of apricot trees, the brother shared a particularly tasty monastic anecdote:

> One day, Brother Jean-François had prepared rhubarb pies. He always tried to save on electricity, and his kitchen was poorly lit. In the darkness, he mistook fine salt for sugar and sprinkled it on the pies. In the refectory, all the monks generously served themselves. From the first bites, we understood …

At the foot of each row of trees, Brother Paul places tansies to repel pest insects:

> This perennial, vigorous, strong plant with intense yellow color is repulsive to insects — aphids, ants, sawflies, mosquitoes, and fleas. Tansy has melliferous properties that feed pollinators — wasps, ladybugs, lacewings, and hoverflies. It emits a camphorlike odor when its leaves are rubbed. Since the Middle Ages, it has been cultivated in monasteries for its effective odor against parasites and to protect meats from flies. However, tansy should not be thrown into compost as it inhibits fermentation.

I was amazed by the monk's arboreal knowledge.

In spring, Fontgombault's orchard is enchanting. The trees sway between pale pink, powdery white, and tea yellow. Brother Paul has a fondness for the sparkling fuchsia color of plum trees. Each flower has a different fragrance. "The plum tree is the delicacy of God," he said. "The pear tree smells bad. The apple tree, however, recalls the old fragrances of Chanel — powdery and delicate."

The lay brother loves working outdoors in all weather. He believes that his Angevin peasant origins influence his love for nature: "The old farmers were true contemplatives."

We passed the statue of Our Lady of Lourdes, sheltered in a niche. Father de Saint-Chamas had delicately arranged this small sanctuary. Brother Paul told me that he likes to pray there for the sick recommended to him. "Our Father Abbot Antoine comes here every day to pray. I often see him around 12:25 [p.m.] because he is perfectly punctual, before the office of sext, he said. "He climbs the path, aided by his cane. He's truly courageous. Before the community branched out to Gaussan, we were ninety monks. We could come see him at any time of the day. He was always available." At that moment, I felt a beautiful emotion in his voice, immense gratitude, so many beautiful memories.

As we headed towards the apiary, the monk stopped in front of old medlar trees: "They say it's the poor man's pear. The monks like it in jam with game. Would you like to taste it?" Indeed, the unknown fruit seemed grainy, sweet, and slightly alcoholic.

"*Ave stillans melle alvearium.*"* The Cistercian sentence was inscribed on the gable of an ancient house at the back of Fontgombault's garden. I thought of the Gospel passage, "The kingdom of heaven is like treasure hidden in a field, which a man found and covered up; then in his joy he goes and sells all that he has and buys that field" (Mt 13:44).

Brother Paul started taking care of the beehives in 1995. "At first, they scared me," he admitted. The abbey has four large hives with twelve beehive frames and seven small ones. They are all populated.

The abbey can produce up to five hundred kilograms of honey per year:

> In good years, we have rapeseed, maple, acacia, sunflower, and wildflower honey. I change my queens every two years. Their birth dates are recorded in my notebook. In the past, queens easily lived for five years. With pesticides today, they are more fragile. In beekeeping, there is

* "Hail, oh hive dripping with honey." One day, during a walk, the prior made this remark to me: "The hive is Our Lady; the honey is Our Lord, and grace."

> a simple principle: It's not men who dominate the bees. Queens or workers do exactly what they want. With them, I admire God's creation a little more every day. I would like you to write that many beekeepers have converted by observing these fabulous organizations.

Brother Paul produces honey in the ancient Trappist honey room. He showed me the filtering machine mixing the elixir that drips from the frames. The year 2019 was disappointing. The abbey harvested forty kilograms of silver linden honey and one hundred forty kilograms of sunflower honey. The monks' consumption was assured for two years, so there was no worry. But Brother Paul remembered that six years earlier production reached peak: five hundred kilograms! That year, his joy was perfect.

The neatly arranged pots lined up by dozens on the shelves. On the floor were half-filled stoneware buckets. "Next year, if the bees can make rapeseed honey, I'll mix it with sunflower," he said. "The taste will be better." Indeed, our monk was as foresighted and organized as his little brides.

Near his "hermitage," Brother Paul melts beeswax, which he mixes with a natural turpentine essence to make polish the monks will use. The lay brother's recipe has been proven: He mixes three hundred grams of wax with four point seven liters of essence. The monastery's furniture, parquet floors, and choir stalls will surely shine: "Our wax is not overpowering." With Brother Paul, time stops, modernity collapses, good scents rise.

He takes care of his bees. In the summer, the worker bees live for only forty days. They die of exhaustion from working so much; fortunately, in winter, their life expectancy goes up to six months. In July, when it gets too hot, he comes to ventilate the hive entrances with a mist sprayer. Beautiful love knows no bounds!

Brother Paul is also the abbey's butcher. It's hard to imagine him slaughtering pigs. Yet, it happens five times a year.

In the old sepia photos of the orchard that Brother Paul wanted to show me before we parted ways, everything was calm, serene, and gentle. I could imagine Brother Paul's friendly bees and thought I recognized some lovely Pinovas, his favorite apples, so crisp and sweet.

XXII
The Dear Cook Who Became Famous

Alongside Brother Paul, Brother Jean-François, and Brother Marie-Joseph, Brother Hervé-Marie works every day, one week out of two, in the vast kitchen of the monastery. The religious cook was born in 1964. Originally from the working-class neighborhoods of eastern Paris, he entered a religious community twenty-two years later before joining Fontgombault in 1992.

Since appearing on a television program dedicated to monastery cooking, Brother Hervé-Marie had somewhat lamented becoming a public figure. On camera, he revealed the secrets of the Charlotte Martin recipe, a dessert beloved by the monks. Since then, he has received letters from France, Canada, even Finland. A charming story circulates in the monastery: One day, a monk, seeing his table neighbors delighting in a cake, remarked that one should not confuse the Fathers of the Desert with the fathers of dessert — undoubtedly, a gentle monastic jest!

In his youth, the brother had never considered embracing the life of a monk. Having become an optician in the Paris suburbs, he had plans to marry and start a family. His path was set.

But the one who diligently attended to the world of eyeglasses for his clients harbored a sadness within. On the June day when I met him in his kingdom, the monastery kitchen, he was willing to talk to me about that distant time. He still doesn't understand the reasons for his past unease: "God's grace is a mystery," he said. "God had sown bitterness over all my joys. I don't even remember the moment I knew I wanted to follow him. I broke off my engagement, and I didn't understand why."

He wanted to become a lay brother to find God in his work. In his mind, the Benedictines worked the land like all good farmers in France. He laughs now at that monastic romanticism that closely resembled the dreams of city boys from Paris idealizing the countryside.

A few days after his arrival, Father Abbot informed him that he would work in the kitchen. The disappointment was great: "At home, we were four boys. Mom made many good dishes. We never took part. I knew nothing about cooking."

At Fontgombault, the stoves are the heart of the matter. Sixty monks and retreatants must be fed. On average, the kitchen produces around a 150 meals per day.

Monastic menus change with the seasons. In summer, a guest might have the chance to taste small wonders: sorrel soup, cold milk soup with monastery mint syrup, vine soup, eggplant omelet, Castilian eggs scrambled with tomatoes and peppers, onion pie, tomatoes and zucchinis stuffed with monastery beef, cold beef with homemade mayonnaise (garnished with chives or parsley), Provencal tomatoes, ratatouille (cooked with zucchinis, eggplants, onions, peppers, tomatoes, rosemary, and tarragon from the garden), the famous Charlotte Martin, baked apples served with quince jelly, apple pies, pear pies, rhubarb pies — all together it's like the wonderful stanzas of an endless gustatory poem

The learning curve on the path of garden flavors was steep. For him, zucchinis and pumpkins had the same color, and he burnt his carrots many times before learning to cook them properly.

In the world, he only knew how to make one thing: omelets. When Brother Hervé-Marie explained to his Father Master that he had the culinary knowledge of a book-loving teenager, the response was: "That's exactly what we need." The young monk felt like he was about to swim in a frozen ocean on a windy day.

In addition to the hours spent at the stoves, he sometimes worked in the garden. Then, after a few years, he was appointed to do the shoe repair and work in the laundry room. Cook-shoemaker-laundryman — that's the extraordinary title of Brother Hervé-Marie.

In 2012, after the takeover of Wisques Abbey, Dom Pateau loaded his plate even more. He asked him to spend a few afternoons doing accounting. However, the monk, who entered Fontgombault in 1992, did not know the new currency, the euro. He discovered the new coins and the pretty bills like a child learning to play Monopoly!

In an abbey, obediences resemble complicated geological layers of earth. They strangely stack on top of one another. Today, among all his jobs, the monk takes a particular interest in his work in shoemaking. He uses leather from the farm's cows: the monastery shoes have long grazed the grass of the surrounding fields.

When the farm brother knows that a cow is going to the slaughterhouse, he asks the shoemaker brother if he needs leather. With his childish, slightly playful humor, Brother Hervé-Marie confessed to me that he had "considerable knowledge of the most sophisticated way to work cowhides." In Fontgombault, the soles are also made of leather, a rare thing, and the stitching is done by hand. Recently, a recognized workshop manager in the sector sought to know the sewers who could make such precise stitches. When he discovered the monk's expertise, he was amazed. The big boss even wanted to hire Brother Hervé-Marie: "He said to me: 'You are one of the last in France to know how to work leather this way. Except for a few master shoemakers for luxury shoes, I don't see anyone else.'" The industrial revolution did not defeat the beautiful work of the Berry Benedictines.

When he leaves his workshop, where the heady smell of natural leather lingers, Brother Hervé-Marie returns to delve into the monastery's recipes. They are carefully recorded in a large black notebook. Brother Hervé-Marie learned a lot from the good Brother Clément, who spent nearly half a century in the kitchen of Fontgombault. The monastic dishes are simple but always tasty. The community needs good sustenance as the days are long and tiring.

The kitchen brothers strive to vary the recipes to please the monks. In summer, on evenings for walks, cold milk soup with garden mint is appreciated. In autumn, baked apples with quince jelly are more fitting. And in winter, the robustness of the pies enchants the monks.

Brother Hervé-Marie has no doubt: The work he does serves his life of prayer. He regrets that the vocation of the lay brothers does not attract more young men: "But God is strong enough to continue attracting new vocations." Recently, several boys have indeed knocked on the door of Fontgombault.

Our lay brother had a military uncle. He used to visit him every year. The man noticed that his nephew had not been promoted. One summer evening, he couldn't help but say: "You don't plan on staying a shoemaker your whole life!?!" The monk's response was unequivocal: "And why not?"

In the past, the names of the lay brothers were often forgotten. They hoed potatoes, picked fruits, scrubbed floors, and nobody remembered them. Memories are less unfair now. However, they more easily remember the faces of intellectual monks and father abbots.

As we parted ways, Brother Hervé-Marie told me with a big smile:

> In a monastery, you don't see anyone anymore. Our closeness becomes mysterious. I've never felt so close to the world since the day I left it. I pray for men, women, children that I've never seen. I know or I guess their sufferings, their wounds: We must be intercessors. A long time ago, when visiting Mont-Saint-Michel with Father Abbot Antoine, I met a little boy. He was with his mom. He asked me who we were with our black habit. I explained our life to him, and I said a few words about God. As I left, I asked him his name. His name was Marin. Every day, I pray for Marin. He doesn't know. We will never see each other again here. But we will meet again in heaven.

XXIII
The Aroma of Good Old-Fashioned Meats

After the office of sext, the monks leave the church in procession. They cross the cloister to reach the refectory. The two abbots lead the silent and solemn march, recognizable by their pectoral crosses.

The refectory dates to the fifteenth century. The characteristic pointed arches of Gothic architecture and the stained-glass windows allow in a white light that gives a gentle grandeur to this room where the monks gather for meals. In winter, the atmosphere is more austere.

The massive oak tables, small stools, dishes, earthenware jugs, and large old white napkins carry a dignified religious air. At the end of the room, above the dais of the abbot's table, a huge Byzantine-style crucifix completes this solemn and unadorned decor.

Opposite these tables, two rows along the walls are reserved for the choir monks. The prior's seat and the sub-prior's, not far from the abbot's table, mark the alignment. Then the monks are placed according to their entry into the monastery. In the middle, facing the abbot who can easily survey his world, is the table for guests and those for lay brothers.

On this Friday in August 2019, many of us took our places at the refectory tables. Yet, we could have been in 1965, 1980, or 1995. Nothing had changed. Year after year, season after season, the tradition governing the meals at the abbey remained the same: The guests wait in front of the unprepossessing entrance to the enclosure, and the guestmaster opens both doors and leads the group, which does not exceed sixteen people, to the cloister wing adjoining the refectory. Father Abbot stands near the door. After greeting the newcomers, he symbolically washes their hands. The novice presents a copper basin, and the abbot pours water from a pitcher over the retreatants' hands. A white embroidered linen cloth is then used to dry them.

That day, as usual, we entered without saying a word. Each discreetly looked at their neighbor, fearing to make a mistake or disrespect the protocol. The monks, impassive and hieratic, stood in front of their tables. Fathers waited near the kitchen doors wearing long white aprons. Their fleeting and circular glances sometimes betrayed a little curiosity.

Each meal followed the same ritual. Every noon, from his pulpit set in the thickness of the wall, a father reads a passage from the Holy Scriptures, a page from the martyrology, and an excerpt from a secular book. During dinners, another father read a section of the *Rule of Saint Benedict*, then an excerpt from a secular book. In early August, the monks listened to reflections by François-Xavier Bellamy from *Demeure*, then those of Cardinal Robert Sarah in *Le soir approche et déjà le jour baisse.**

Father Abbot opened each lunch with the famous injunction "*Benedicite*!" ("Bless!"), to which the monks also responded "*Benedicite*!" Then, Dom Pateau continued by saying: "Oculi omnium," and the community followed, "*In te sperant, Domine, et tu das escam illorum in tempore opportuno: aperis tu manum tuam, et imples omne animal benedictione. Gloria Patri et Filio et Spiritui Sancto.*" ("The eyes of all creatures hope in you, Lord, and you give them their food in due time. You open your hand, and you fill every living being with blessings. Glory to the Father, and to the Son, and to the Holy Spirit.")

In the evening, he began the meal with this prayer: "*Edent pauperes*," and the brothers sang: "*Et saturabuntur, et laudabunt Dominum qui requirunt eum: vivent corda eorum in saeculum saeculi. Gloria Patri et Filio et Spiritui Sancto.*" ("The poor will eat and will be satisfied, and those who seek the Lord will praise him; their hearts will live throughout the ages. Glory to the Father, and to the Son, and to the Holy Spirit.")

Sometimes, the reading of the *Rule* might bring a smile to the guests, but the monks took the matter seriously. Such as during the dinner when the serving monk read chapter fifty-five entitled "The Clothing and Footwear of the Brothers":

> Clothing suitable for the conditions and temperature of the places they inhabit will be given to the brothers, as they require more in cold regions and less in hot countries. The abbot must take this into consideration. However, in temperate places, a cowl and a tunic suffice for each monk, with a scapular for work. The cowl will be furry in winter, light or worn in summer. Sandals and shoes will also be given to cover the feet. The monks will

* François-Xavier Bellamy, *Demeure* (Paris: Grasset, 2018); Cardinal Robert Sarah, with Nicolas Diat, *Le soir approche et déjà le jour baisse* (Paris: Fayard, 2019).

not be concerned with the color or coarseness of these various items but will be content with what can be found in the country they live in or procured at a low price. As for the size of the clothes, the abbot will ensure they are not too short but fit each person. When new ones are received, the old ones will always be returned at the same time and will be deposited in the wardrobe for the poor. It is enough for a monk to have two tunics and two cowls, to change them at night and have them washed. Anything more is superfluous and should be removed. The brothers will also return the shoes and everything that is worn when they receive new ones. Drawers will be given from the wardrobe to those who must travel; they will return them upon their return, after washing them. The cowls and tunics will be slightly better than those they usually wear. Before leaving, they will receive them from the wardrobe and return them upon their return. For beddings, a mattress, a sheet, a blanket, and a pillow will suffice. The abbot will often inspect these beds, fearing that there might be something someone has appropriated. And the one in whose possession something not received from the abbot is found will be severely disciplined. And so that this vice of ownership is cut off at the root, the abbot will provide everything necessary — namely, a cowl, a tunic, sandals, shoes, a belt, a knife, a stiletto, a needle, a handkerchief, tablets — to remove any excuse drawn from necessity. However, the abbot must always consider this sentence from the Acts of the Apostles: "They were given to each according to their needs." Therefore, the abbot will consider the needs of the weak and not the bad will of the envious. He will remember, in all his decisions, that God will take them into account.

In the refectory, too, each monk dines "according to his needs." No more, no less.

A few days later, on Wednesday, August 7, lunch started with leftover soup, followed by potatoes with Swiss chard, ending with sweet cakes served with jam. In the evening, another serving of leftover soup, soft-boiled eggs, ratatouille, and apples from the orchard.

On Sundays, like feast days, the table became more plentiful. For Sunday lunch on August 11, we had carrot soup, homemade country pâté, braised beef from the farm, tomatoes from the garden, candied fruits served with pears and syrup-soaked mirabelles, and freshly baked shortbreads. For dinner, a hearty soup, green beans, semolina porridge with raisins accompanied by Brother Paul's succulent honey. The farm, gardens, and orchards of the monastery abundantly provided what the world would kindly call "organic" food.

The meal was always taken in silence. However, the ballet of the serving monks coming and going with the dishes created a slight hubbub. At their tables, the monks turned into gentle automatons. They served themselves from large cafeteriastyle dishes, lifted their cups, tasted the food, and neatly folded their napkins. On his platform, Dom Pateau presided with either a frank smile or the disapproving look of a good family father. Next to him, Dom Forgeot revealed no emotion.

Life in the refectory is punctuated by the liturgical calendar. Saint Benedict prescribes his monks to observe a monastic Lent from September 14 to Easter.

The practice of fasting dates to the early days of Christianity; it was already observed among the Jews. The early monks fasted to rid themselves of passions and foster the spiritual life. The early Christians fasted on Wednesdays and Fridays, and two days before Easter the fast was absolute. The days of preparation for Easter gradually increased over the centuries, reaching forty days between the end of the fourth century and the beginning of the sixth century.

At Fontgombault, the monks take three meals on non-fasting days. Abstinence is no longer perpetual. During the monastic Lent, the monks fast every Friday. During Advent, they fast on Wednesdays and Fridays. During Lent, they fast every day except Sunday.

On August 10, two monks had the honor of a beautiful bouquet of garden flowers placed at their seats. They were named Laurent. For each patronal feast, the monks are honored in this way.

At the end of lunch, we listened to the obituary of the abbey. On the eve of the anniversary of their death, the reader reads a short biography of the deceased former monks of the abbey written in Latin. Behind the tables, the monks focused, prayed. Memories, images, and scents returned. Most often, too, a certain joy.

After the final praises, the porter, the sacristan, and the guestmaster, impassive, left the refectory, followed by the retreatants, while the monks disappeared into the kitchen. A cohort was busy in front of the large sinks serving the dishes. Half an hour later they would walk in the countryside. A first group would stop in a sunny pasture amidst the vineyards. Other monks sat in the wild herbs of the sunken roads for good laughs. Some fathers had sun-kissed complexions, some lay brothers were paler. There was no rule, for once.

Soon, they would have to return for none, the ninth-hour office of the day.

XXIV
"Satisfaction!"

On this beautiful autumn day, during lunch, the monks came in procession to kneel before Father Abbot's table. The scene was amusing, fascinating, curious. The parade seemed endless. A father or brother approached, bent his knee, bowed his back, remained for a moment, then left. We were enjoying a good vegetable soup, the fish was coming, and the monks continued their strange ballet.

That very morning, the chapter of faults had been held in the presence of Father Abbot. After prime every Friday, the monks publicly declare their failures in observance and poverty before the community to ask for forgiveness from their brothers. Dom Pateau then decides on the appropriate penalty. Most often, satisfaction in the refectory, or recitation of a prayer.

"To make satisfaction" is a phrase derived from the Latin *satisfacere* ("to do enough"), already found used by the third-century theologian Tertullian and used to speak of the penitence of men toward God. *Satisfacere* and *satisfactio* are terms found in the language of law. In the Church, they have taken on a precise theological meaning: *satisfacere* is indeed "to do penance, to repair, to atone."

Satisfaction is a voluntary act. *Satis facere* means to do enough to compensate for the damage caused. The penalty becomes satisfactory when it is voluntarily assumed by the guilty party to compensate for the fault.

In monastic tradition, the term is already found used by the monk John Cassian, who died around 435, and the idea is as old as monasticism itself: If a brother commits a material fault, he must repair his fault, most often by prostrating himself in the oratory before the community, until the superior signals him to get up.

Saint Benedict adopts the expression and its use. In the forty-sixth chapter of the *Rule*, he writes:

> When someone, in a task in the kitchen, the cellar, in a workshop, the bakery, the garden, in the exercise of a trade, in any place, makes a fault, breaks or loses something, or commits any offense, if he does not immediately come of his own accord to give satisfaction and confess it before the abbot and the community, and if it becomes known through another, he will undergo a more severe correction. But if it is a secret sin of the soul, he should confess it only to the abbot or to the elders experienced in spiritual life, who know how to heal their own wounds and those of others without exposing or divulging them.

The founder of the order clearly distinguished the internal forum and the external forum, what belongs to the domain of conscience and what belongs to the public domain. The faults for which the brothers publicly accuse themselves at the chapter of faults are only of this second category.

Practically, one first distinguishes the small satisfactions, which are done spontaneously at one's spot; the monk kneels and gets up by himself. This is the case, for example, for minor faults in singing, errors in solfège, rhythm, or text. For greater satisfactions, the monk comes to kneel before the superior and waits for his signal to get up. They are done when the monk arrives late to the office or the refectory, for more considerable faults in singing — for example, a mistake in intonation that would break the beautiful harmony of the choir, or in penance for the accusation at the chapter of faults.

The satisfactions for faults concern only faults against poverty: a monk breaks or damages an object, tears a garment; forgets to turn off a light when leaving the room; wastes water, electricity, gas, or food; spills a dish; uses heating with windows open... The Benedictines are pioneers: The harm to good use and respect for nature, which the monks must never forget, are part of the faults they accuse themselves of. At Fontgombault, ecology is no joke.

Similarly, the monks accuse themselves of unnecessary purchases or violations. A monk once told me most wisely: "We live in a society that is losing the sense of true justice. Today it's not seen, not caught; not caught, not punished; if caught, hanged." For a Benedictine, and a Christian, the true sense of justice coincides with a sense of responsibility.

The monks do not seek suffering. Dolorism, which consists in wanting suffering for its own sake, with a morbid spirit, is a deviation. Dom Jean Pateau had enlightening words on this subject:

> It is wrongly thought that it is suffering that saves, since it hurts, and we are thwarted in our tendency considered

> bad. But the Christian sense of suffering consists in transfiguring the suffering we did not want, but which we are obliged to endure, by the love with which we offer it. The true perspective of salvation is that of love. Suffering becomes the revealer of this love, as in chemistry or photography. Love is a gift. Instead of enduring or rebelling, if we offer suffering, we open our hearts to love.

In a monastery, any fault, even involuntary, disrupts some order. A brother who arrives late to the office, even if "it's not his fault," alters an objective order. By kneeling to ask for forgiveness for his delay, he offers compensation. According to Dom Prior, "satisfaction has an afflictive dimension, which concerns the order of justice and wants to repair the fault by the penalty, and an affective dimension, which is of the order of love." The brother repairs the objective order of justice by satisfaction, and also the interpersonal order of love when this satisfaction is offered willingly. What matters most is not the amount of the penalty, but its inner quality, the way it is experienced both for the present and as a stimulus for the future through the desire to do better. In faults against observance, one is apparently on a purely objective level, but it is up to everyone to refine their sensitivity toward God and the community by making these satisfactions acts of charity. Thus justice is preserved and at the same time transcended by the order of charity. The spontaneous aspect of satisfaction is emphasized by the fact that at the chapter of faults the accusation comes from oneself, and not from others.

A monk wishes to be responsible. He must answer for his actions and take responsibility if he has caused any harm. The abbot added:

> This implies recognizing an order of objective values that surpasses and measures us. Relativism leads to ar-

> bitrariness and absolutism. Something, a value, is only relative if it is in relation to something else. We must indeed come to an absolute because, as St. Thomas Aquinas said, "one cannot go back to infinity" in the chain of relationships. If everything is relative, everything becomes absolute, in an arbitrary manner. Often, the conduct of a community becomes difficult when a monk absolutizes something that is not. Speaking of responsibility, autonomy, and freedom should not lead to a resignation or a failure of authority: A monk is responsible for his obedience and for how he participates in the authority of the superior through his obedience. Let's go further: The common good is not the sum of individual goods; it refers each one to his responsibility toward the safeguarding of the integrity of the whole body. All members of the community, each at their level, are responsible for the common good, which is ultimately life in charity and union with God, beyond all its more visible aspects. To obey as well as to make satisfaction for a fault belong to this responsibility of each toward the common good.

Yet, monks are also likely to get used to the chapter of faults and miss the opportunity to take responsibility. This can happen at any moment in the brothers' lives. The demon of routine is never far away; nor is the sadness of acedia.

At Fontgombault, numerous anecdotes are reported about faults and satisfactions. Around twenty years ago, two American priests visiting asked Father Barais, the sacristan, about the chapter of faults: "Is it true that in the chapter of faults the guilty monk kneels in the middle of the room, in silence, surrounded by three or four brothers who vehemently accuse him while pointing at him?" To which Father Barais replied with his laconic and inimitable deadpan humor, "In Hollywood, maybe!"

Similarly, during a meal, the monks heard a terrible clatter of pots and pans in the kitchen. They then saw a long procession of several servers and cooks come to make satisfaction in turn, smiling from ear to ear!

And how not to laugh thinking about this novice who made so many satisfactions at matins that the novice master instructed him to make only one per page of the breviary. Gradually, he began to make fewer mistakes. Sometimes, several weekly chanters or cantors simultaneously make a mistake in the intonation of a piece, prompting Father Abbot to give a mallet strike, or causing the complete cessation of the choir's singing. In this case, there can be a small cascade of satisfactions from five or six brothers.

The loudest story, however, did not immediately lead to a great satisfaction: The small accompanying organ, perched above the choir, has a wooden cover to cover the keyboard. An organist had placed it precariously at the top of the spiral staircase that leads to the instrument. At the very beginning of solemn vespers, in the presence of a bishop, the cover slid and went down the stairs to the bottom, hitting each step with a loud noise. The organist could not make satisfaction since he had to continue playing. But it happens: When he makes a mistake in his notes at Mass and the choir cannot start, he goes down to make satisfaction at the first opportunity.

It also happens in the choir that a father accidentally lets his stall fall back. The seat is mounted on a hinge, which makes a loud noise. There is then great satisfaction.

In the refectory, a brother who drops his stainless-steel tumbler while taking it out of the rack under the table makes satisfaction — and it is not uncommon for the reader to stop abruptly if the noise is too loud. However, if an object is dropped without noise, there is no satisfaction.

Sometimes, a server accidentally drops a dish or a serving spoon, or the cutlery of a guest while serving. This makes enough noise to trigger a great satisfaction. These are just a few of the anecdotes that have been related to me. As time passes, everything becomes lighter, and the monks turn these satisfactions into good-natured jokes. During walks, memories are quick to resurface.

The atonement for faults, a sort of general amnesty that Father Abbot offers several times a year, especially during major festivals, is an important time in the life of the monastery. All accounts are reset to zero — an act of mercy that finds its full meaning at Easter.

The Benedictine is far from the Jansenist posture described by Georges Bernanos in *The Diary of a Country Priest*: "It seems to me that at the first consciousness of himself, man would fall back into dust." Alas, we tend to think that monks share this melancholic pessimism, this sterile way of covering themselves with soot, of constantly ruminating on our human poverty. We are committing a small mistake in judgment here ... and Dom Jean might well ask for "satisfaction"!

XXV
Never Tire of Praying

St. Anthony the Great, the father of monasticism, often said that a monk should love God every day as if it were the first. At eighty-seven, Dom Antoine Forgeot has never stopped putting this advice into practice: He never tires of praying. For "God is tireless, and his mystery is unfathomable," he repeats.

How does one maintain the joy and grace of pure love? On the day of my last meeting with Dom Forgeot, his words disconcerted me: "We seek nothing. We must approach God like a child in wonder and put everything in its place. Everything is secondary, except for God." So, should we only love heavenly things and despise earthly matters?

The Benedictine monk seeks to make his prayer a gentle habit. It structures his day, provides markers, and pacifies the heart. The Desert Fathers explain that monks strive for continual prayer, being in God's presence at every moment. The term "continual prayer" might be misleading: "It's not about reciting formulas," insisted Dom Forgeot. "Once the soul has truly risen to God, it doesn't want to come back down."

Each monk has his practices. The freedom he enjoys is real. But he must embrace the devotions encountered in the monastery. It's more about discovering and following God's path than creating a program in one's image. "When one knows God, one realizes his magnificence. One can only love him," says the former father abbot. Hope comes at this price.

Dom Paul Delatte speaks of the "white sanctity" of the Benedictines. For him, everything is naturally balanced by the *Rule*. The master of Solesmes writes:

> Some souls may be extreme in poverty, mortification, zeal, or a kind of supernatural fervor. … These are what people see most clearly and imitate most easily. … Alongside such prismatic sanctity, there is a white sanctity, where all tints blend into perfect simplicity and equality. It makes less of an impression; it's less noticeable, and the inattentive might not notice it at all.*

The white sanctity of the sons of Saint Benedict is silent, discreet; no one can see it except God.

What happens if a monk is no longer able to pray? Dom Forgeot's response left me speechless: "He must continue to pray. Never stop." A monk who realizes that he is being distracted in prayer is already part of the way back toward God. A few seconds of prayer can suffice. Each moment spent recapturing his imagination is a step closer to God.

A monk doesn't learn to pray as he labors over Latin. There are no written tests: A monk truly prays when he's unaware of it. For Dom Forgeot, a monk shouldn't wonder if he's praying

* Dom Paul Delatte, *Commentary on the Rule of St. Benedict*, op. cit.

well. He shouldn't question his prayer. God is his only judge. If a monk tries to assess his prayer, he might quickly become discouraged. Cassian quotes Saint Anthony: "There's no perfect prayer if the monk notices himself praying."

The Abbot of Fontgombault offered a comparison:

> Prayer is a bottle thrown into the sea. The monk loses ownership of the moment, of time, of usefulness. He dedicates himself to the useless, without even expecting a tangible encounter. Prayer demands a leap of faith. It's cast into the unknown. But it remains in expectation. Sometimes, light comes. More often, God remains silent. In praying, we are certain that we are in his sight and that we are loved.

The monastic life is so given that the monk prays continuously without being aware of it. The gift is difficult. In a letter to Alain Fournier, Charles Péguy wrote that "the worst is to have a soul hardened by habit. On such a soul, grace can do nothing. It slides off like water off an oily fabric. ... Such respectable people do not soak up grace."

"Grace obeys special laws. It takes root in wounded hearts that wish to open," Dom Pateau said. "To progress in the spiritual life, one must start from where we are, not where we wish to be. To advance, one must accept their past. Grace beautifies the soul. A heart that gives is a heart that is ground: It becomes porous."

The monk doesn't pray just to pray. He needs this constant exchange between his heart and God's. He awaits a response. But prayer that becomes a challenge is misguided.

Love cannot be kept in a box. It must be continually nourished. The essence of monastic life is in the present moment, sustaining the monk's love for God. He puts the past in perspective and doesn't worry about the future. The present moment is the time to respond to God. A monk who strays from the present can no longer encounter God. Accepting the present is accepting God. It's in the present and its concrete activity that God's presence is revealed.

One day, a monk from Fontgombault shared with me a beautiful text about prayer. The young monk did not wish me to reveal his name, fearing to break what he poetically called "the King's secret":

> It is very difficult to talk about prayer. Father Jerome, a Trappist from the Abbey of Sept-Fons, rightly says that one can easily tell if those who speak of prayer actually pray or are merely repeating things read in books. After ten years of monastic life, I am beginning to glimpse what prayer might be. I probably pray, but it's a real labor, to be started repeatedly. It seems to me that to pray is to remain calm in the hands of God. A Carthusian monk said, "Contemplation is the art of being calm." These words are profoundly true. To pray is not to tire of peering into the night of God. This does not mean that there is never any light, but one must consent to the mystery and listen more than look. Vision is reserved for heaven; here below, one must "incline the ear of one's heart," as Saint Benedict says in his Prologue, quoting Scripture. The entire framework of our prayer, the Divine Office, the Rosary, all the prayers are there to soften our hearts, to open them, to make them attentive to the voice of God. But I should rather say that we must become attentive to the silence of God. It is said that true music leads to silence. Beyond the Word of God, we must learn to listen to His silence. Saint Hildegard said that God is a "silent music." It is not poetry: The

> strongest friendships are not the most talkative. How can one be capable of wasting time with the Friend? I think of Cardinal Sarah and Brother Vincent.* To pray is the same: to stay hand in hand with God. You might say that everything then passes through the gaze. In the company of God, everything passes through the peace of the heart. That's why the ancients insisted so much on the purity of the heart. It's not about purity in the "primary" sense of the word, but about the clarity of crystal that lets all the light pass through. Today's society sorely lacks intimacy. Our life of prayer is our life of intimacy with God. It concerns only us, in the end, and that's why the experience is difficult to share. We need a guide to show the way, but whether through the words of a man or directly in the secret of the soul, this guide is always God, and each one advances alone with him. In the pretty words of Dom Roux, one must know how to stay "alone with the Alone."

The difficulty in praying occurs at any age. Often, there is nothing dramatic about it. We are far from the dark nights of the faith of the great mystics. The monk never really understands the origin of his disturbance. He knows that slackness in small details has delicate consequences. Sometimes, he may have difficulty entering the literary form of the Psalms: Fatigue, passing anxieties, routine lead him to be less attentive when reading these long poetic texts of the Old Testament. He must become again like a little child who repeats the same words over and over to understand and love them. Even in darkness, there is always a ladder: God puts on the monk's lips words that become richer the more

* In the spring of 2016, young Brother Vincent from the Abbey of Lagrasse passed away prematurely due to sudden multiple sclerosis. During the last two years of his life, when he could hardly communicate, he became friends with Cardinal Robert Sarah. I had the honor of recounting their touching story in my book *A Time to Die*.

he repeats them.

Monastic life is a royal path. But what path is it? The monk strives to dedicate himself to what is essential. As time passes, he becomes more successful at it. He repeats the same prayers at the same hours. In secret, each day, they are different.

The community accepts all weaknesses, including those in the life of prayer. Contemplation is not a mathematical exercise. A monk can progress, regress, fall, and rise again; mastery is never perfect. There are sometimes terrible coalitions: The choir is weaker than usual, the day's work is mediocre, the cold is harsh or the heat oppressive, sleep is difficult, and prayer becomes a trickle of lukewarm water.

The novice learns to speak to his master as to a doctor. He must rid himself of all pride, bashfulness, and shyness to open his heart and soul to him. A patient who hides things from his practitioner prevents him from finding the right remedies, and they lose precious time.

In the Fontgombault family, custom has it that the abbot is the spiritual father of the monks. But the monks however are free to choose [a director of conscience]. Throughout his life, the monk remembers that, according to the teachings of the elders, opening one's heart is the remedy for many temptations and a sure path toward progress.

In the monastic day, there are hundreds of opportunities to draw closer to God. Yet habituation hides in the smallest corners. I was struck by hearing a monk say:

> The monk who makes [the] Sign of the Cross too quickly is a monk in danger. There are sometimes pious distractions. But self-renunciation must prevail. Similarly, the beginning of the vespers service is daunting. The monk has worked all afternoon and must suddenly rediscover the taste for contemplation. He has a few min-

utes of standing time in the cloister to regain the peace necessary for true prayer.

The Benedictine must constantly keep death in mind. "What presumption to imagine that God would not have decided otherwise," a young monk told me. "Perhaps tomorrow we will no longer be of this world. We must simply remain with God."

In contemplative life, habit is a necessity, an ascetic practice, and a risk. When a monk recites the Hail Marys of the Rosary, the line between passive habit and active prayer is thin. He must monitor himself to make good use of the habit. It is both a trap and a strength. The monk's prayer is not just the fruit of his training within the monastery walls. It also comes from his past life. The monk prays as his parents might have taught him. Spiritual heritage exists.

Habit is a matter of love that draws the monk toward the Infinite. In a monastery, the interior life is simplified. All monks resemble one another: They respect the same Rule, the customs and traditions of the monastery. Yet, in their relationship with God, each one is unique. A monastery is a warm greenhouse where a man can grow spiritually. He is protected by the enclosure from all external aggressions. When a monk receives the habit, the master gives him the key to the abbey, signifying that he will never be a prisoner of the monastery. The monk can leave Fontgombault as he wishes, but he cannot return without the key.

Similarly, when illness does not prevent them, monks receive the Sacrament of the Anointing of the Sick in the chapter room. This sublime gesture marks the importance of the unity of the community in prayer until the end of life, just as, when a monk is close to breathing his last, they gather around the dying man's bed.

The monks would like to be able to communicate the fire

that inhabits them. But first, it is not their vocation. And, moreover, when they have the opportunity, the exercise is almost impossible. The Benedictine is a man who has simplified his life so much that his essence becomes incommunicable.

I remembered a passage from the Gospel of Saint Paul that my friend Cardinal Robert Sarah likes to quote:

> Likewise the Spirit helps us in our weakness; for we do not know how to pray as we ought, but the Spirit himself intercedes for us with sighs too deep for words. And he who searches the hearts of men knows what is the mind of the Spirit, because the Spirit intercedes for the saints according to the will of God.
>
> We know that in everything God works for good with those who love him, who are called according to his purpose. (Romans 8:26–28)

And he adds, to make the simplicity of prayer clear, "What could be more beautiful than a faithful dog who falls asleep at the feet of his master, knowing he is loved?" The monk's prayer is as trusting as that of the faithful dog.

Amor

A young person who wishes to enter the monastery seeking personal fulfillment or self-realization is on the wrong path.

We are approaching the ultimate lesson of the monks. These men do not have a way for finding happiness. The last words of Dom Jean echo as a solemn and friendly warning:

> The modern dictate of happiness, elevated to the status of a dogma, has become so suffocating in our modern societies that it makes life sad. Psalm 27 tells us: "The LORD is my light and my salvation; / whom shall I fear?" The monk seeks nothing. It is only God that we seek. Saint Benedict provides this criterion to the master in the prologue of the *Rule*: "Does the novice really seek God? — *Si vere Deum quaerit*?" The brother who seeks heaven is ready to renounce himself to truly implement "the very powerful and glorious weapons of obedience." At the beginning of a religious life, a misunderstand-

> ing can arise. The temptation to create for oneself a comfortable life puts the monks in a touchy situation. In that case there is no gift. An illusory and temporary success might follow. But God does not call us to self-realization; he calls for a servant, a witness, a martyr. The door to happiness requires passing through the trial of the cross. True happiness is communion with the Risen One. If so many consecrated lives wither, it is because communion has been and is still lacking. The joy here is God.

How can one say goodbye to Dom Jean, Dom Antoine, Dom Jean-Baptiste, and all the good monks of Fontgombault? The kindness of Father Abbot, his extraordinary way of finding the spiritual part in every man, the unaltered fidelity of the emeritus abbot at the end of his monastic life, whose every word is a balm, the generosity of Dom Prior, his courage so lacking in our time, these beautiful memories, could they ever fade from my memory? That is impossible: One never really leaves an abbey where the heart has received so much.

The brief exchanges, here and there, with Father Philippe; the warm conversations at the porter's lodge with Father Bernard; the enchanted walk in the orchards, where Brother Paul reigns; the discovery of Father Florian's humanism, Father Damien's uncompromising intelligence, and Father Guillaume's sensitivity were blessings, rare and blissful moments.

For a long time to come, the Benedictines of Fontgombault will remain as those I have met. The fragile silhouette of Dom Antoine, the hurried air of Dom François, the deep gaze of Brother Raphael-Marie, the mischievous smile of Brother Charles-Marie, the sly eye of Brother Hervé-Marie, the overflowing sincerity of Father Pierre-Antoine will not fade. They are not characters of a novel, but monks who have given their days to God.

Thomas Merton spoke of monastic life by describing "a silent and mysterious communion between man and his brother, between man and all of creation."* Benedictines are dead to the world, but they understand it with a sharpness that could make many powerful people bend. It's an unsuspected strength. The sons of Saint Benedict live in the present. They need nothing else. That is enough to form a united and fraternal family, joyfully looking at the things of life.

In turn, let us look simply at the life of the monks, observe these wise children — it will already be a great step.

Often, I have left Fontgombault full of sadness. A bitterness, a melancholy, a pain came to contradict my happiness. Returning to the world became a journey toward a *terra incognita*.

My fault would have deserved "satisfaction"! The monks do not abandon us. They pray incessantly for us. They pray day and night. They pray at the beginning of their religious life and in the final hours. In the rain or the sun, on stormy days, on frosty days.

They pray to God. They love us.

* Thomas Merton, *Silence in Heaven*, trans. Marie Tadié (Paris: Arthaud, 1955).

Since You Are No Longer Here: Letter to Dom Antoine Forgeot

On Saturday, August 15, you left us. You departed. You went toward God. From now on, every August 15 of our lives, we will think of you.

I was in Lagrasse when Cardinal Sarah announced the sad news to me.

I remained speechless for a long time. Sad, yet, already joyful.

You were an exemplary father abbot, a gift from God. Some might have criticized your inflexible rigor. Alas, what a sad time. What spiritual poverty in these weak souls who no longer understand the unmatched greatness of ascetics.

I can never express enough how much your humility has marked me. It radiated. It covered everything. Moments with you were blessings. A thousand things come back to my memory. I remember your wisdom. Your humor, too. One day, you wrote me a message on the back of a ballot paper for the 2017 presidential election. It was a ballot for Jean-Luc Mélenchon. You had commented: "A monk does not like to waste paper."

In June 2020 we met for the last time. And we talked about *Great Happiness*. A few weeks later, I returned to Berry, but I did not want to bother you. You seemed tired. Your step was slow. Your eyes sunken. In the refectory, we exchanged a glance, and you gave me a beautiful smile. I still see it. I will see it for a long time.

At the beginning of this literary adventure, I timidly asked you to be in this world when my book would be released in bookstores. You had replied, "One can never know!" To be honest, I was not very pleased with that answer. And, I can't say why, but I suddenly had a doubt.

On the evening of your death, Dom Jean Pateau, your dear successor, said to me: "Dom Antoine has bargained with the Holy Virgin." The expression was surprising. He meant to tell me that you had asked Mary to come and fetch you, like Dom Édouard Roux, the first abbot of Fontgombault. The mother of Christ granted both of your requests.

On the night of Wednesday, August 12, 2020, the emergency services came to the abbey to take you to the hospital in the small town of Le Blanc. But you never returned to Fontgombault which you had entered sixty-seven years earlier. Sixty-seven years of fidelity. Sixty-seven years without ever leaving the path.

Dom Antoine, you will be missed. You will be missed by the monks of Fontgombault. You will be missed by Dom Jean

Pateau. You will be missed by a vast crowd. But, up there, with your brother Xavier, whom you have found again, you watch over us. For eternity.

Nicolas Diat
Lagrasse, Thursday, August 20, 2020